gypsy
butterfly
GW01605590
rocket
milk
The answers are at the back of the book
desert
fisherman
Eskimo
web
tadpole
bread
bird

Designed and produced by
Grisewood and Dempsey Ltd Elsley House,
24–30 Great Titchfield Street, London W1

Published by Purnell Books
Berkshire House, Queen Street, Maidenhead
ISBN 361 03875 5
Printed and bound by
Vallardi Industrie Grafiche, Milan

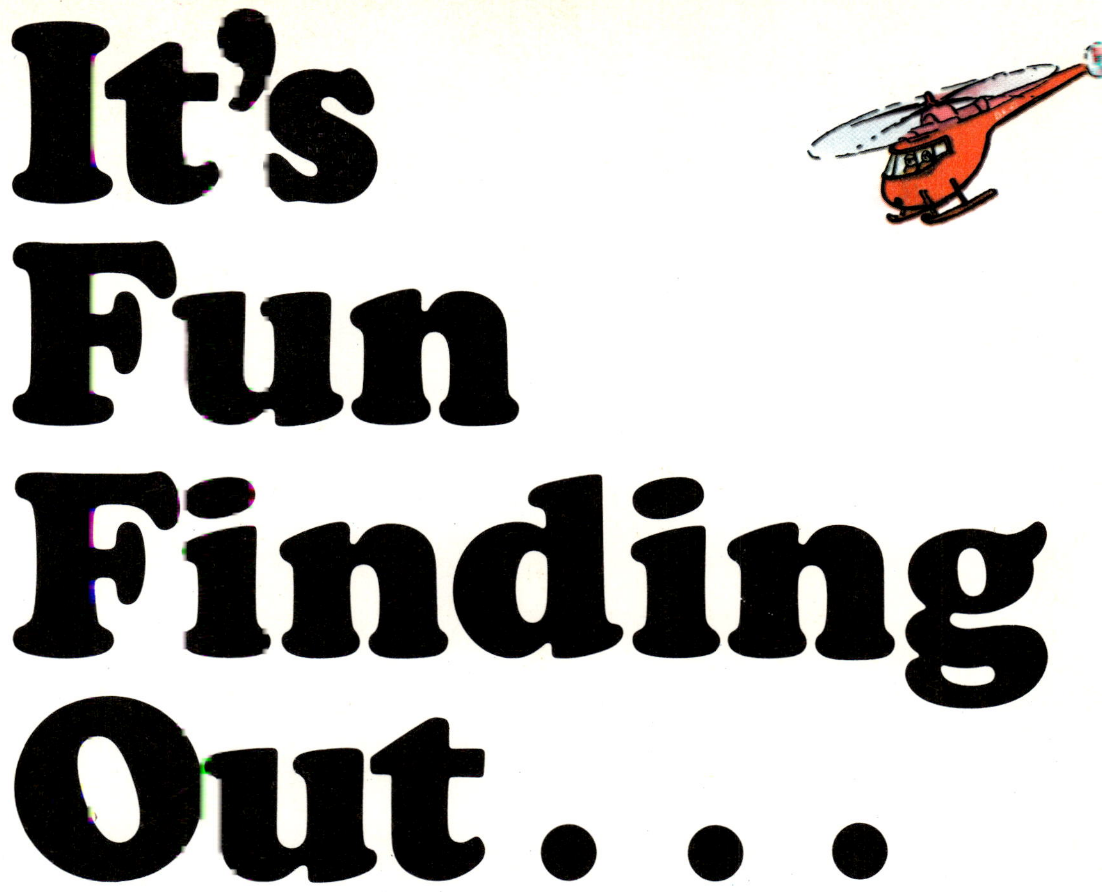

It's Fun Finding Out . . .

Edited by
Deborah Manley

Illustrated by
Moira and Colin Maclean
and
Kailer-Lowndes

PURNELL

CONTENTS

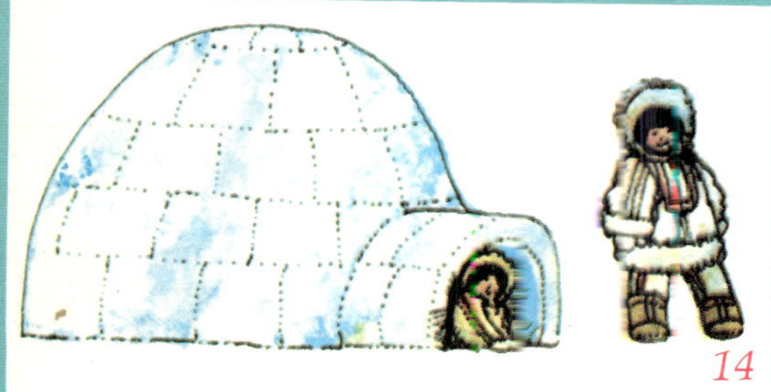

Our world is made up of all sorts of places

On open plains there are large farms.

In hot, wet lands there are jungles.

In cold lands there is lots of snow.

What makes the weather?

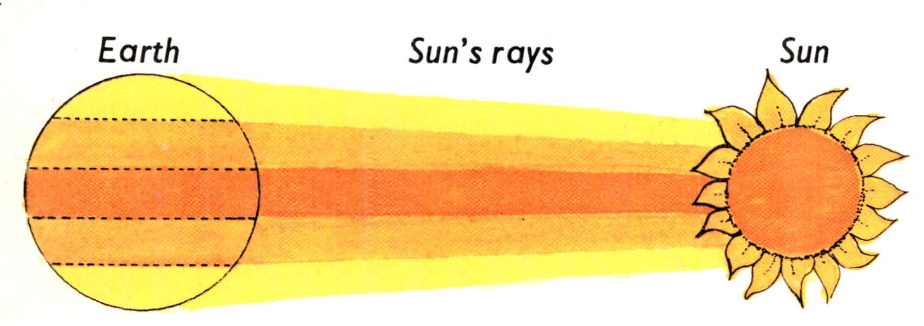

The sun shines on our Earth from far, far away.

Where the sun shines most it is hottest.
Where the sun shines least it is coldest.

The usual weather for each part of the world throughout the year we call the CLIMATE.

In high places it is colder than in low places.

In some parts of the world there are four different seasons.

Why does it rain?

The sun heats water. It evaporates and rises.

The water cools and makes clouds.

There is so much water in the clouds that it falls as rain.

The rain water flows back to the sea.

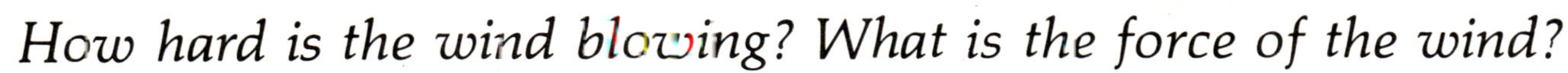

How hard is the wind blowing? What is the force of the wind?

Force 0: Smoke rises

Force 1: Smoke drifts

Force 2: Leaves rustle

Force 3: Flags flap

Force 4: Twigs move

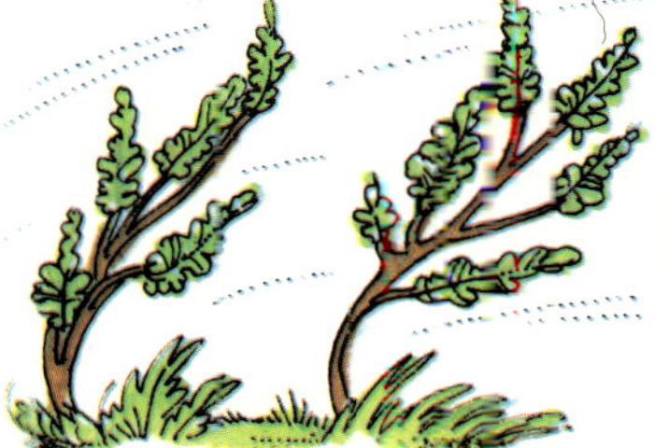

Force 5: Saplings sway

Force 6: Branches sway

Force 7: Trees move

The instruments we use to measure weather

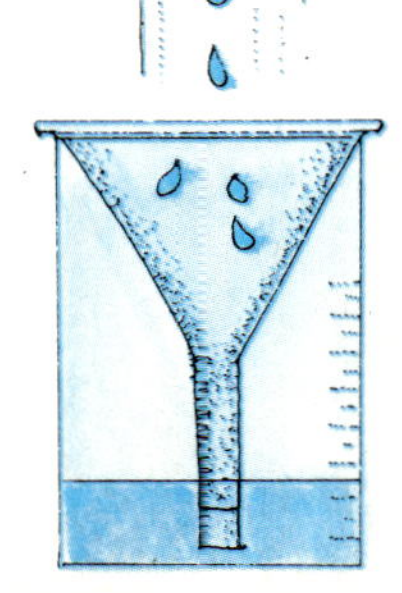

A rain gauge measures rain fall.

A thermometer tells how hot it is.

A weathercock tells which way the wind is blowing.

All around the year

Day and night

What makes day and night?

The Earth is like a ball going around the Sun.
As the Earth goes around, it turns
round and round too.
On the side toward the Sun, it is day.
On the side away from the Sun, it is night.

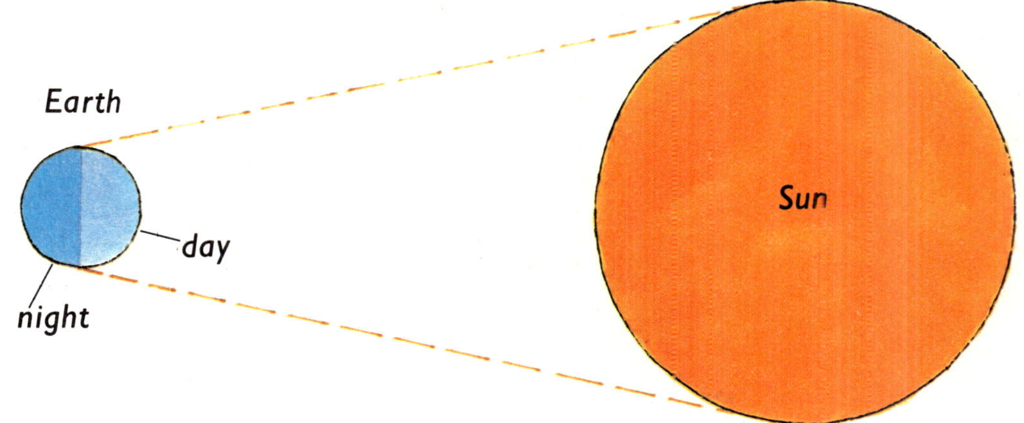

There are 12 months. In Britain, it is coldest at Christmastime.
In warm southern countries like Australia, it is hot in December.

There are 4 seasons:

January

February

March

July

August

September

Make your own day and night

You need:

Fix the thread on to the ball with the drawing pin.
Turn on the torch in a dark room.
Twirl the ball round in the beam of the torch.

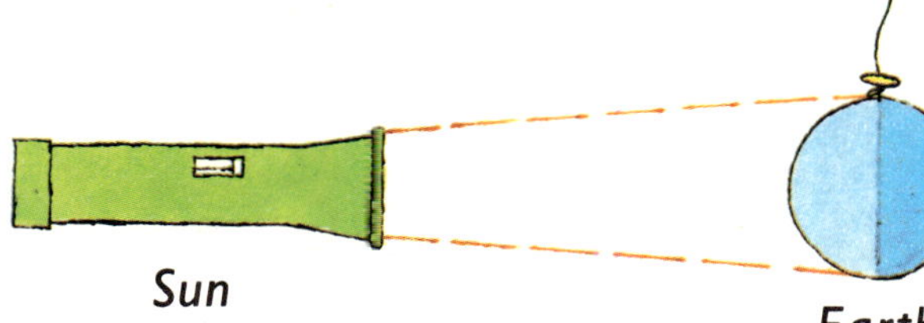

The days of the months

Thirty days has September,
April, June and November.
February has twenty-eight alone.
All the rest have thirty-one.
Excepting Leap Year,
that's the time
When February's days
are twenty-nine.

The days of the year.

There are 365 days in a year, except in a Leap Year when there are 366 days in a year.

It is Leap Year every fourth year.

Spring	Summer	Autumn	Winter

April

May

June

October

November

December

Homes in many lands

Dutch houses by a canal

A few people still live in castles.

A Swiss chalet in the mountains

An Indian tepee in America

A house on stilts in Borneo

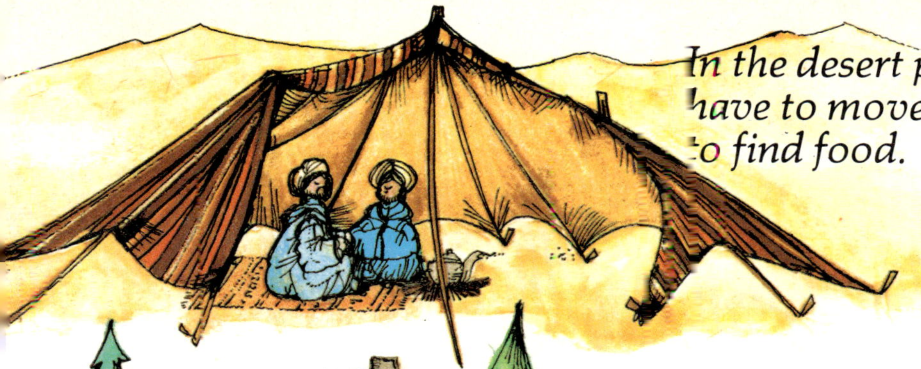

In the desert people have to move around to find food.

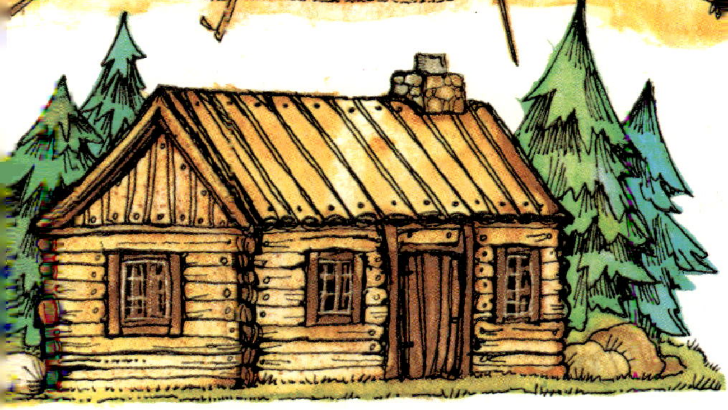

A log cabin in the forests of Canada

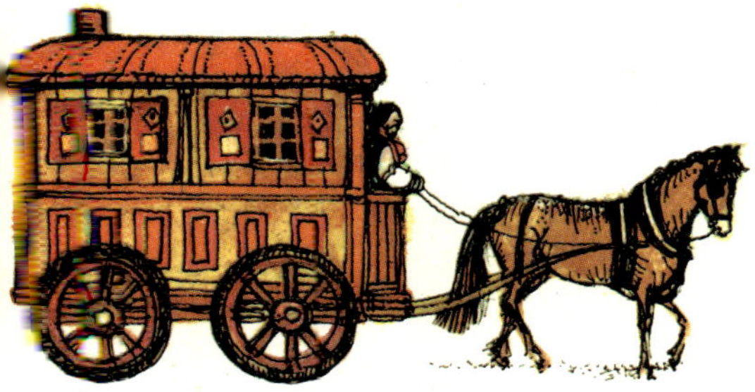

A gypsy caravan

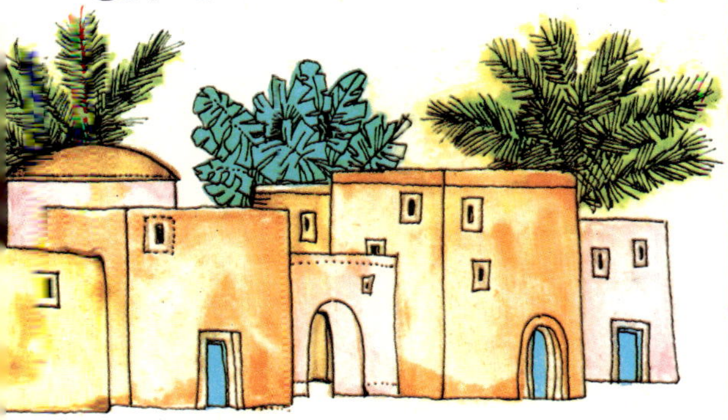

Houses in North Africa have thick walls to keep them cool.

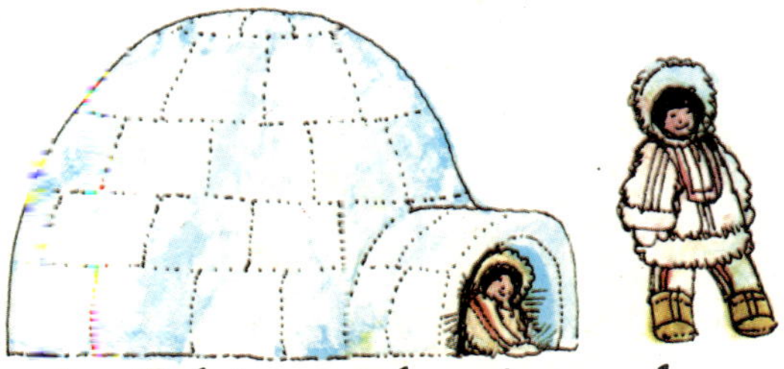

An Eskimo igloo is made from blocks of ice.

This man has nowhere to live.

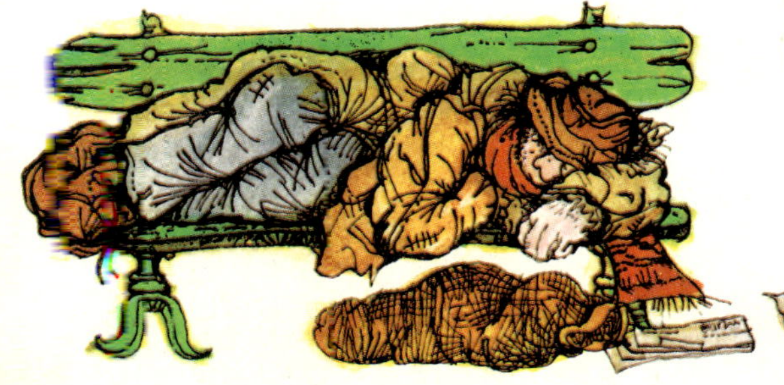

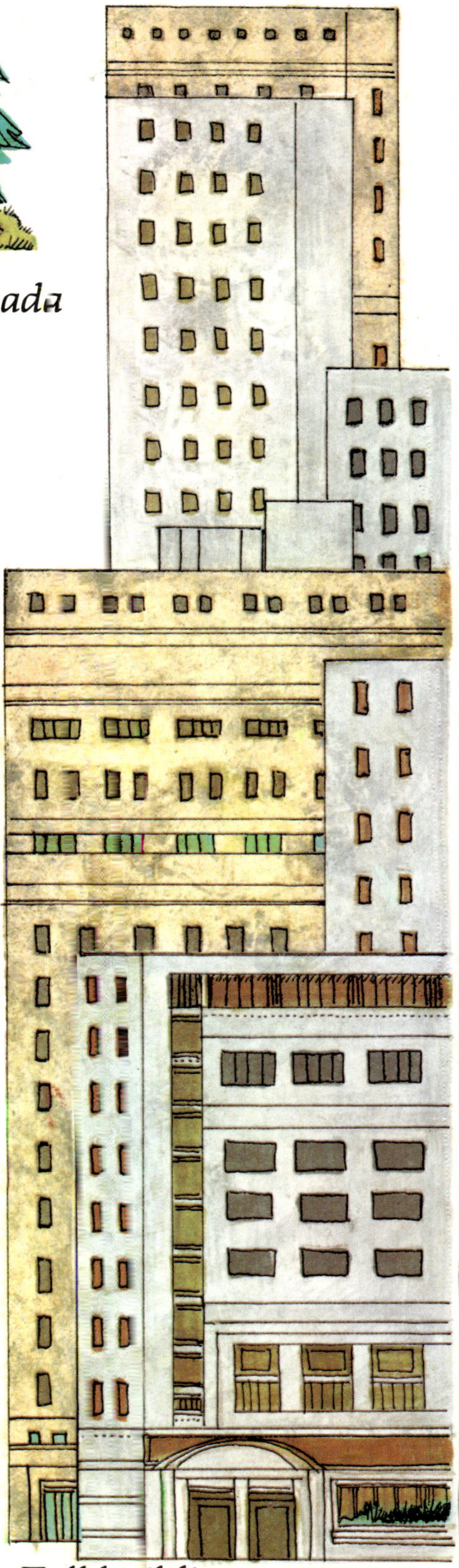

Tall buildings save space in big cities.

What are houses made of?

logs

planks

steel girders

mud blocks

bricks

cement

tiles

ice blocks

cloth and skin

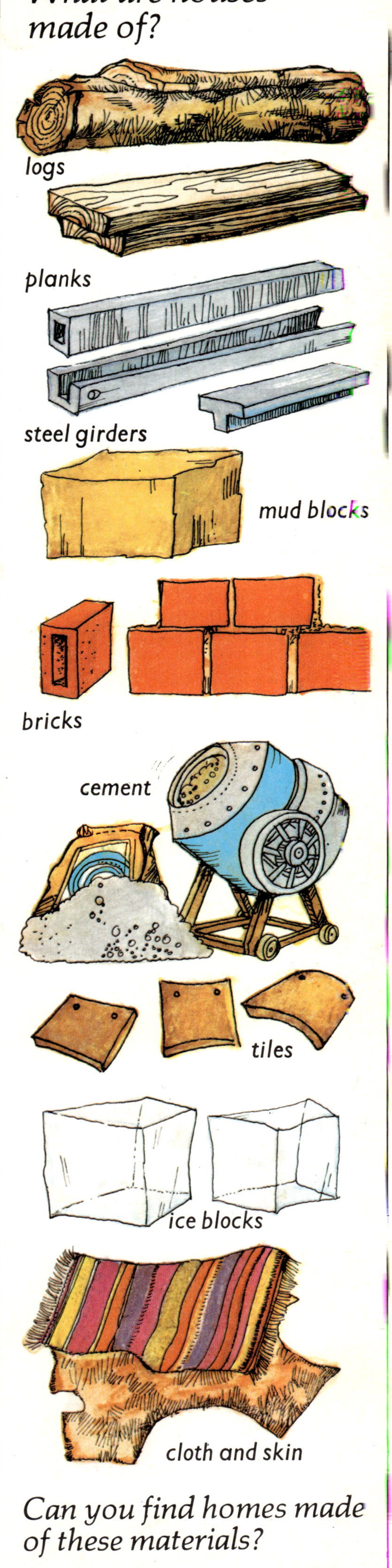

Can you find homes made of these materials?

How a house is built

The site is cleared and levelled.

The architect draws a plan of the house.

The foundations and walls are built.

The bricklayer joins the bricks together with mortar.

The roof is put on and the window frames are put in.

The carpenter makes the roof, the window frames, the floor and the stairs.

Water, gas and electricity are put in by plumbers and electricians.

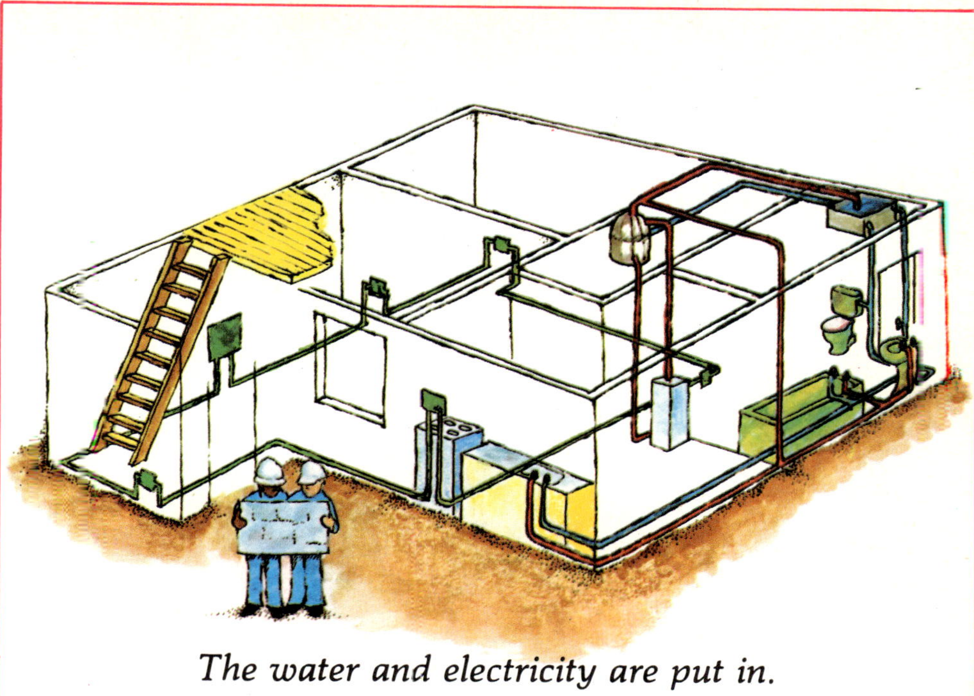

The water and electricity are put in.

The decorators use these tools and materials.

The house is decorated inside and out.

We use these tools to make the garden.

The house is ready, but the garden still has to be made.

The clothes people wear

Some people wear special clothes to do their jobs.

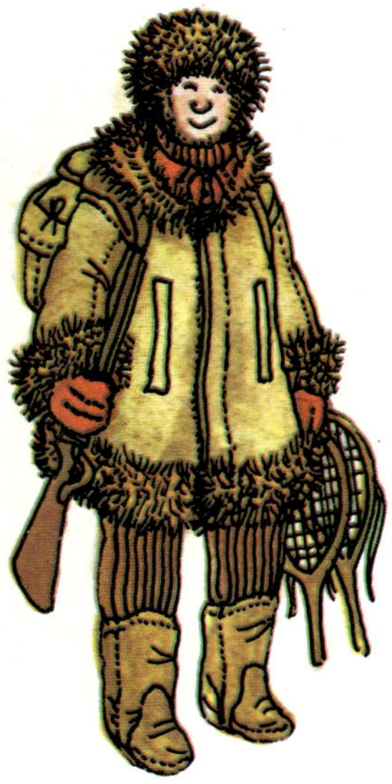

trapper

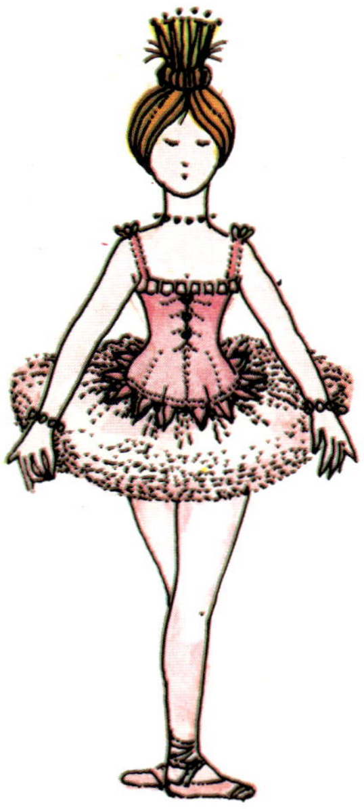

ballet dancer

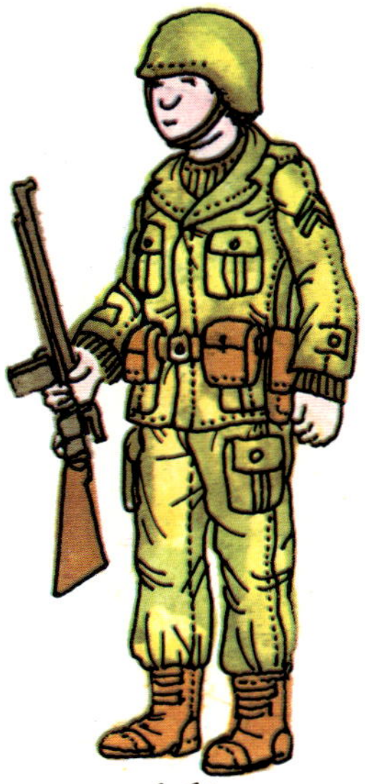

soldier

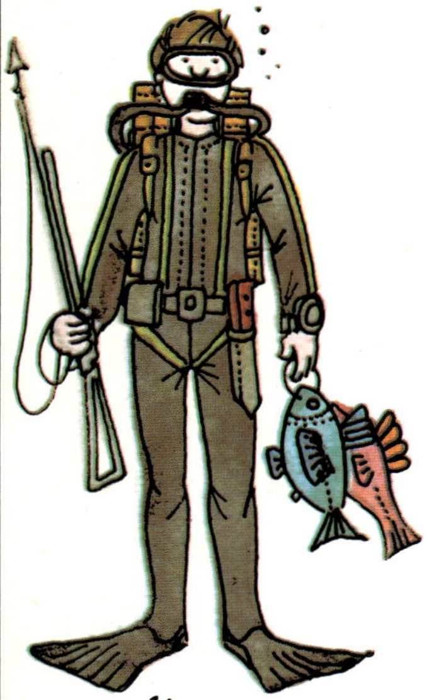

diver

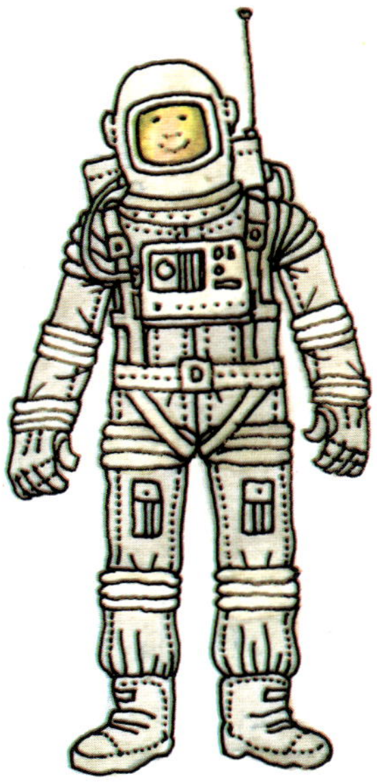

astronaut

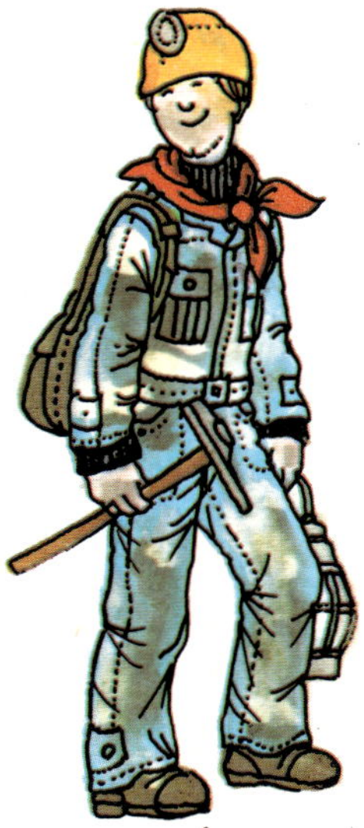

miner

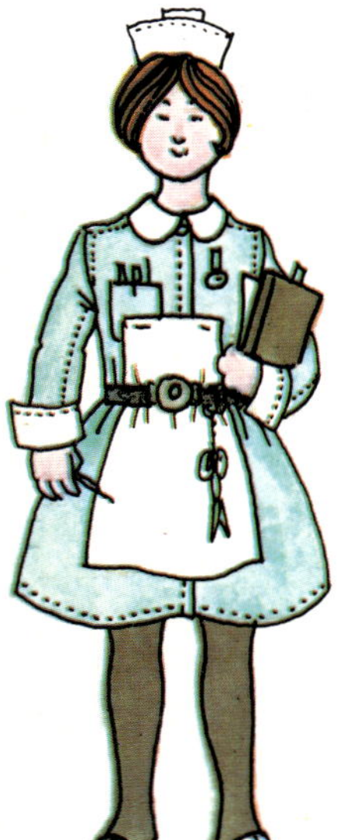

nurse

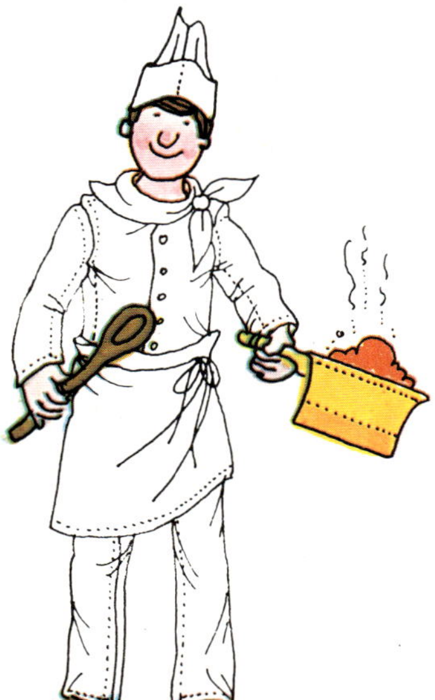

chef

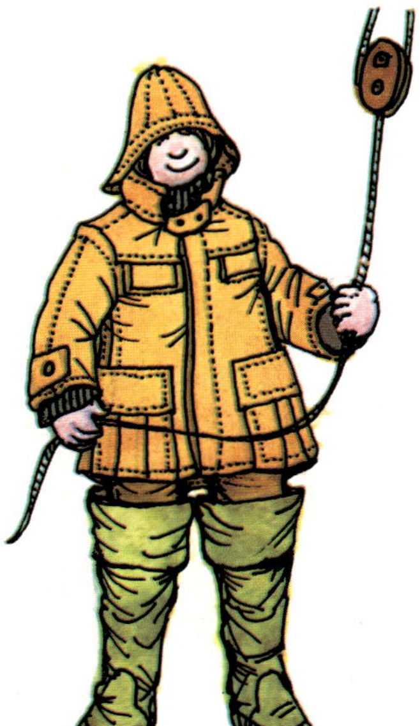

fisherman

Eskimo

Austriar

Burme

Russian

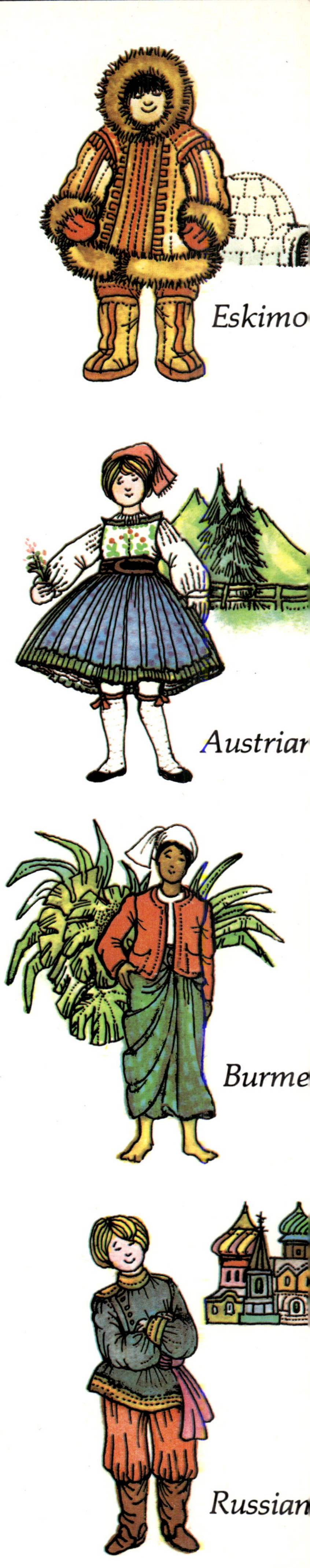

People around the world

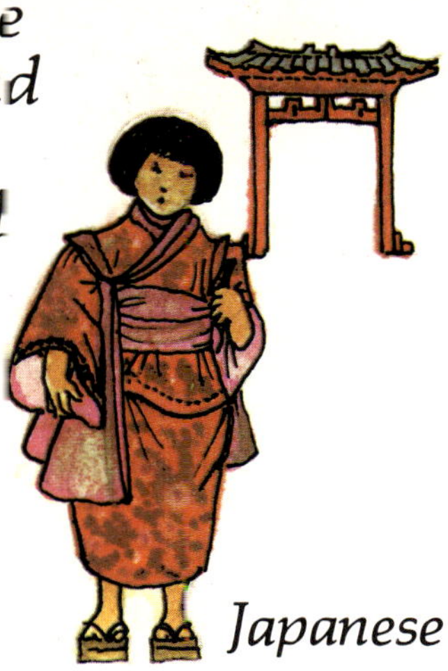
Japanese

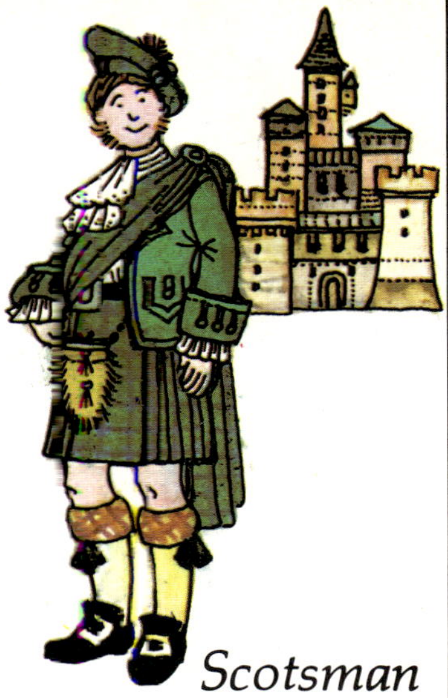
Scotsman

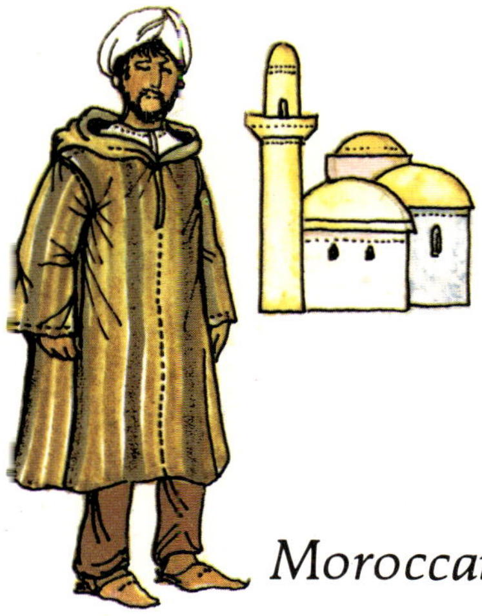
Moroccan

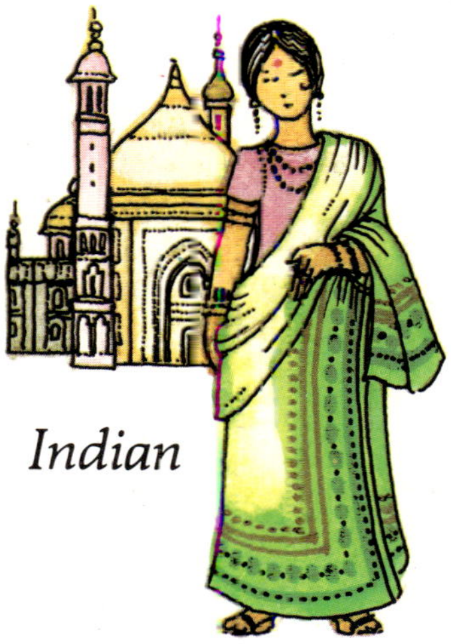
Indian

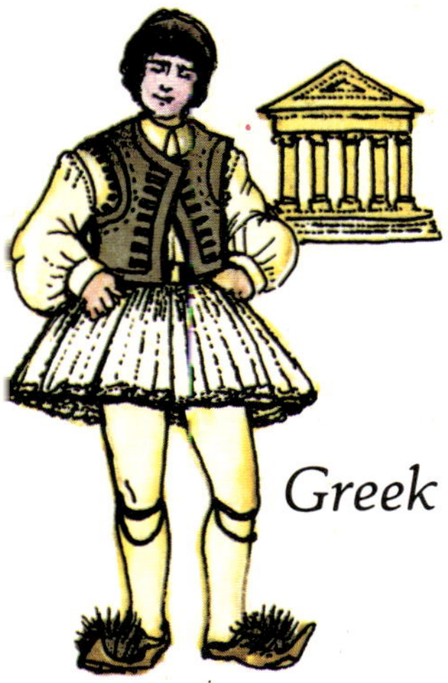
Greek

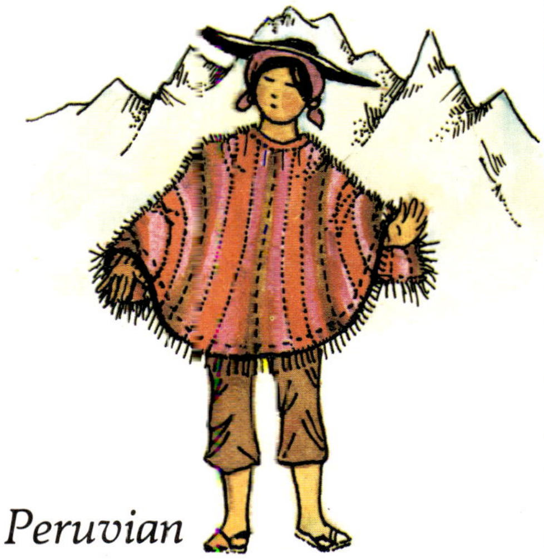
Peruvian

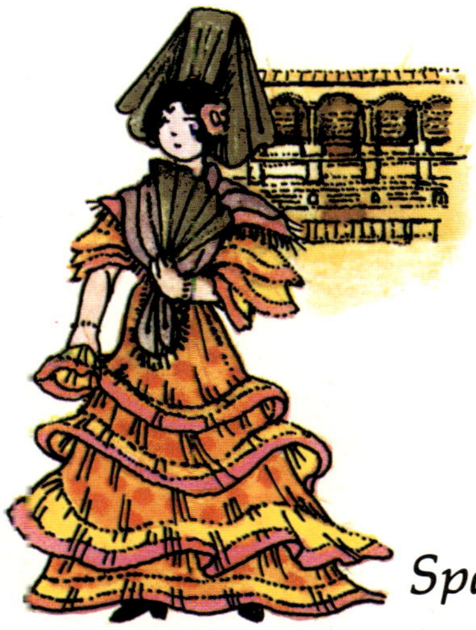
Spaniard

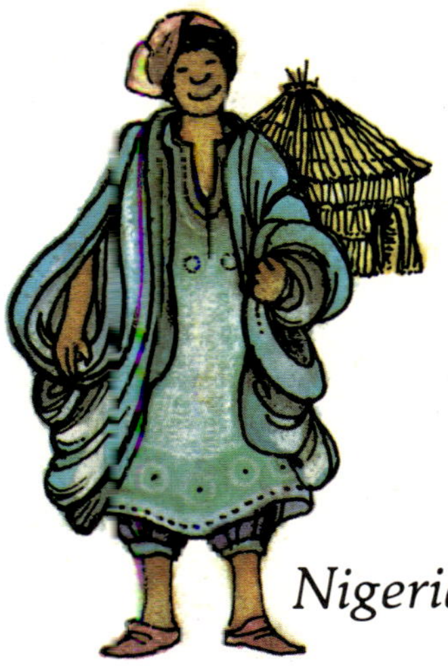
Nigerian

Make your own fancy dress

Pirate

Queen

Cowboy

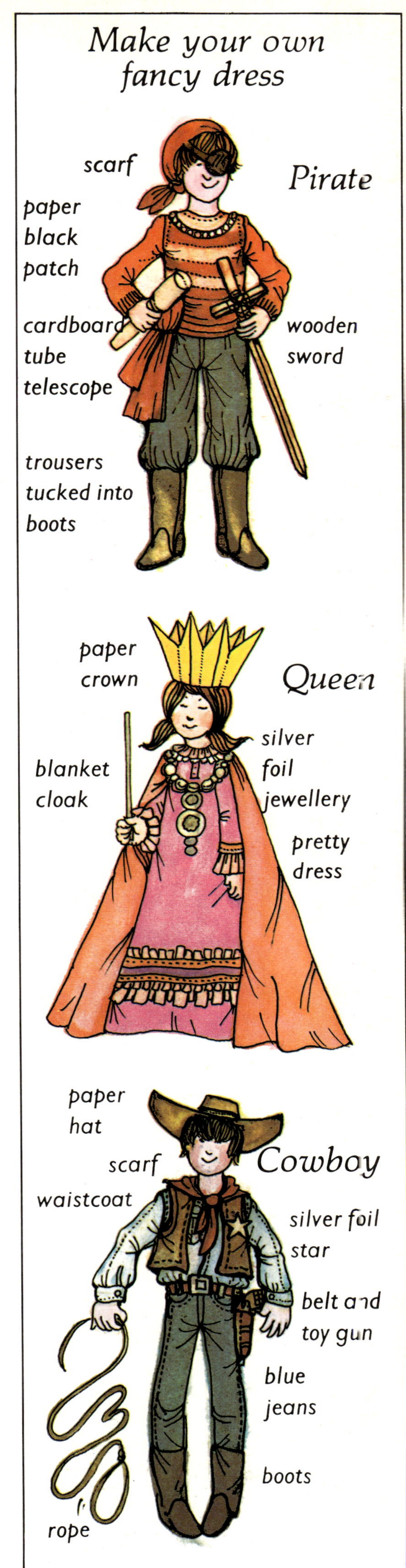

The animal world

Animals are divided into two large groups.
Animals with backbones are called vertebrates.
Animals without backbones
are called invertebrates.

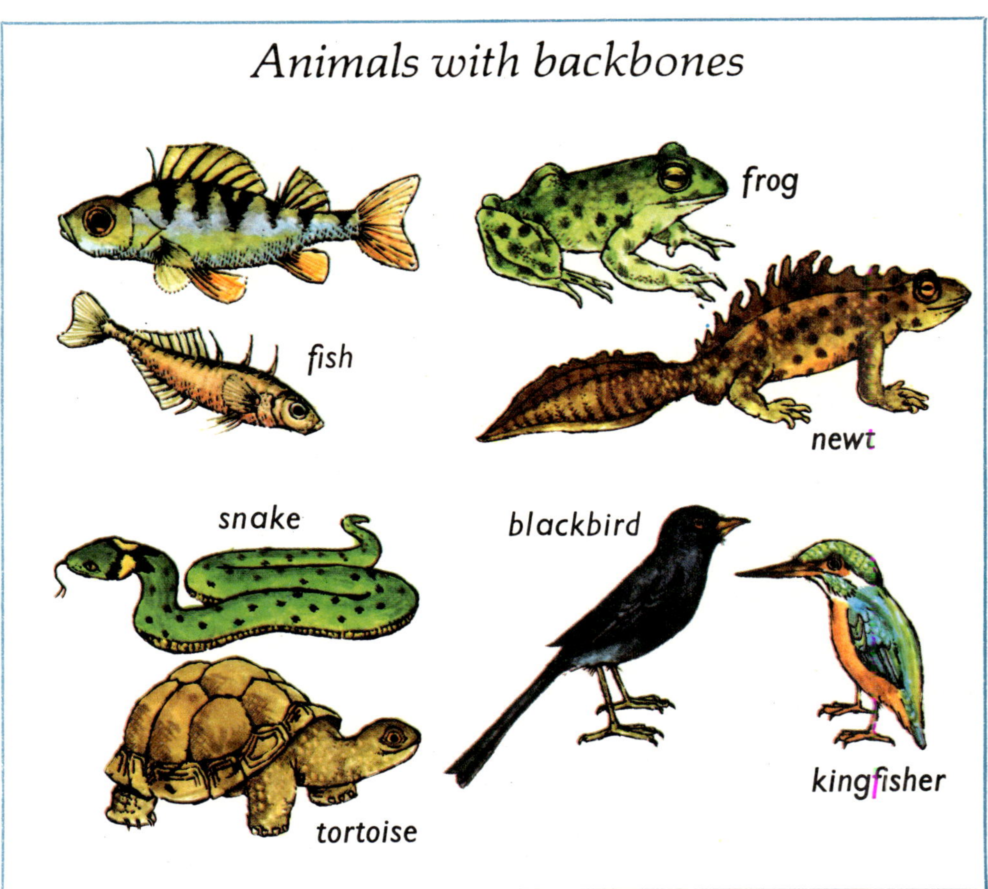

Mammals are animals with backbones too.
They feed their babies on milk.

Porpoises are mammals which live in water.

Bats are mammals which can fly.

Within each group of animals there are animal families.

Here are some of the cat family.

You belong to the same family as the apes.

gorilla

orang-utan

chimpanzee

gibbon

boy

girl

Animal homes

Beavers cut down trees to build their lodges.
They dam the river to make a pond.

Birds make nests to lay their eggs in.

Some animals sleep through the cold winter.

How many animals can you find living around this tree?

Looking at birds

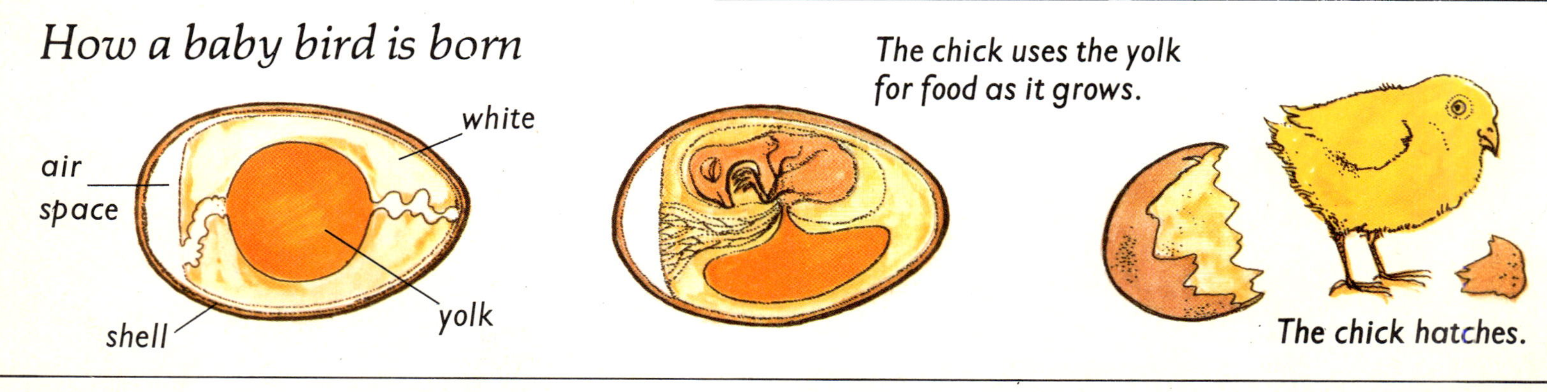

The owl's great eyes help it to see at night.
Swallows fly away in winter to warmer places.
The magpie likes to steal bright things.
Seagulls catch fish in the sea.
The heron wades on its long legs to catch fish.
The woodpecker pecks holes and searches for insects.
The kiwi cannot fly.
The grebe carries its babies.
It spreads its wings on the upstroke.
How a bird flies
It pushes its wings down to lift itself.
It lowers its wings and jumps.

The world of small creatures

Can you find 20 small creatures?

1 dragonfly
2 moth
3 butterfly
4 wasp
5 bee
6 ladybird
7 grasshopper
8 daddy-long-legs
9 stick insect
10 caterpillar
11 spider
12 fly
13 snail
14 ant
15 lizard
16 frog
17 stag beetle
18 slug
19 centipede
20 earwig

How a spider makes a web

The spider builds a frame of thread.

It spins spokes across the thread.

It spins a coil of sticky thread to catch insects.

The life of a butterfly

Worms at work

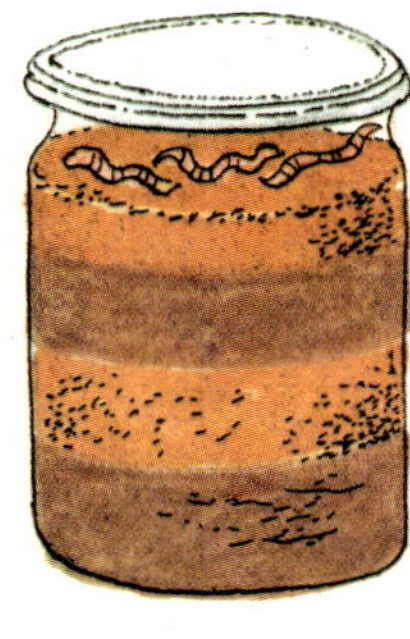

Fill a jar with layers of damp soil and sand. Put some worms into it. Cover the jar for a week. Look to see how the worms have mixed up the soil.

Life in an ants' nest

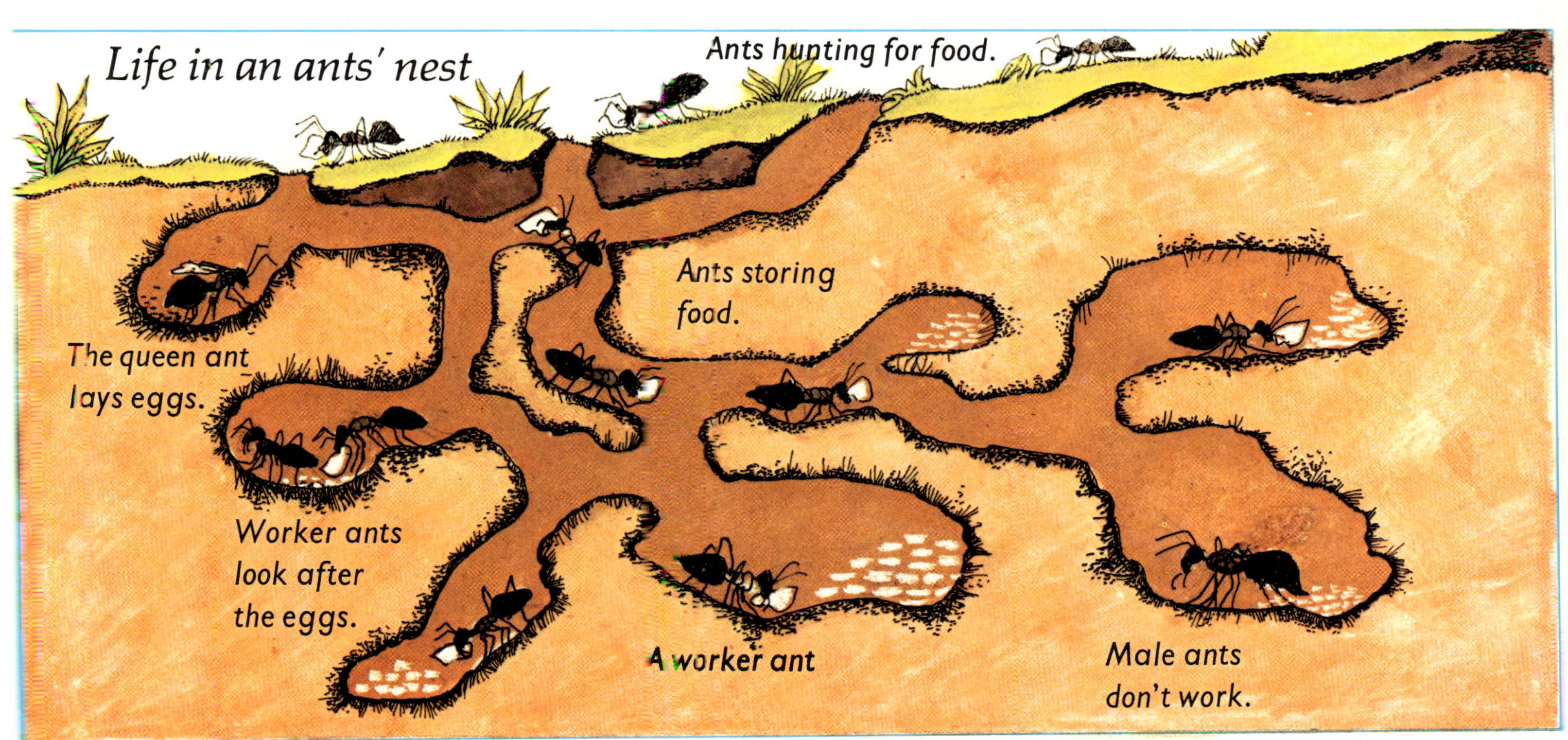

How a tadpole grows up

Some extraordinary animals

When a skunk is attacked it gives off a terrible smell.

The peacock fans out its tail to attract the peahen.

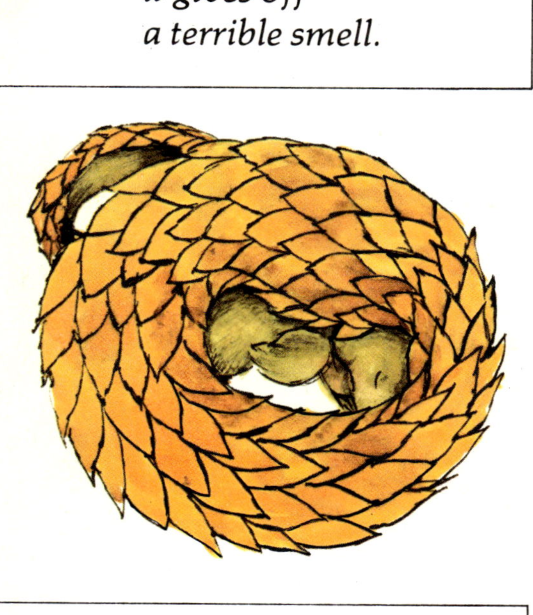

A pangolin can roll itself up in a ball. It can hang from a tree by its tail.

The sloth eats, sleeps and moves around upside down.

The puffer fish puffs itself up to frighten its enemies.

The blue whale is the biggest animal in the world.

Strange animals from Australia

The lyre bird copies all the sounds it hears.

The mother kangaroo carries her baby in a pouch.

When a lizard is caught by its tail, it can drop it and escape. Soon it grows a new tail.

Puffins build their nests in burrows.

All sorts of dogs

There are many different breeds of dogs.
People breed dogs to do different things.

Working dogs

Working dogs help on the farm.

Gun dogs

Gun dogs help hunters.

Looking after your dog

1 Give your dog food and water.

2 Take him for plenty of walks.

3 Brush him well and keep him clean.

4 Teach him to do what you tell him.

5 Love him.

Terriers
Scottish Terrier
Bull Terrier
Fox Terrier
Cairn Terrier
Terriers were bred as rat catchers.

Hounds
Greyhound
Dachshund
Basset Hound
Afghan Hound
Harrier
Hounds hunt
and race.

Pet dogs
Pekinese
Chow-chow
Mongrel
Maltese Terrier
Poodle

The Wolf Hound is the
biggest dog.
The Chihuahua
is the smallest dog.

3

4

5

Animals at work

Animals work for us in lots of different ways. They help us to do heavy work. They give us food to eat and wool to make our clothes. They help us in many other ways too.

These animals carry heavy loads for us.

oxen

donkey

llama

camel

elephant

huskies

Some animals give us things to use.

Sheep give us wool.

Hens give us eggs.

Cows give us milk.

Yaks give us milk too.

Some animals help us in other ways.

This dog guides a blind person.

At the circus, this seal makes us laugh.

This cat catches mice in the barn.

This dog guards his master's house.

Why the camel can work in the desert.

There are many different kinds of horses which work for us.

Palomino

Clydesdale

Arab

Percheron

Shetland pony

Life under the sea

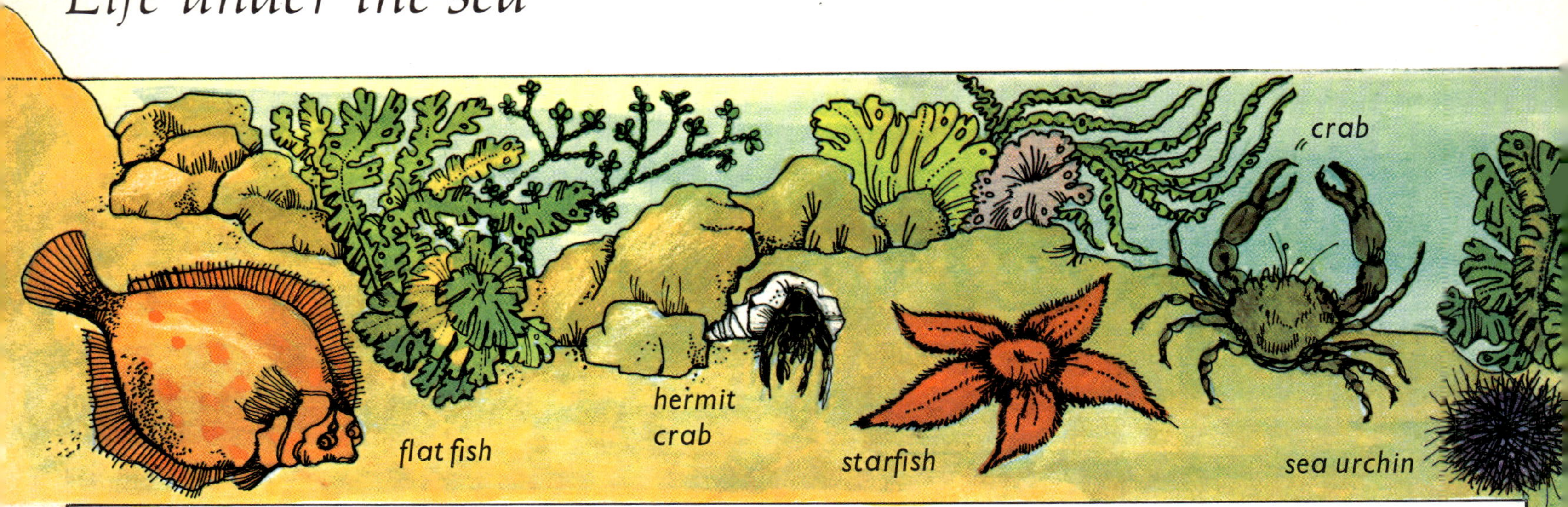
crab
hermit crab
flat fish
starfish
sea urchin

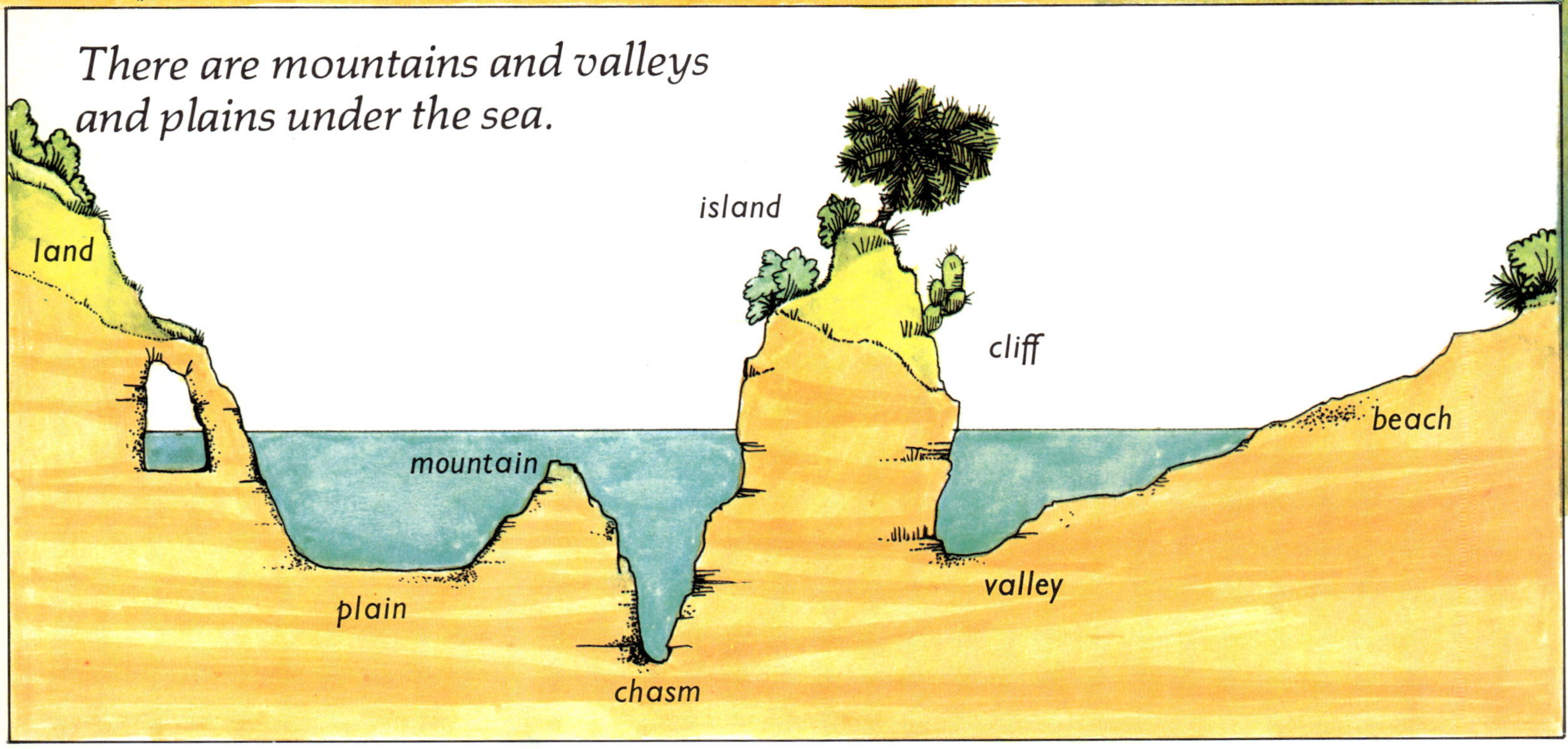
There are mountains and valleys and plains under the sea.
island
land
cliff
beach
mountain
valley
plain
chasm

The tides

Every day the sea comes up the beach twice and goes down the beach twice.

High tide

Low tide

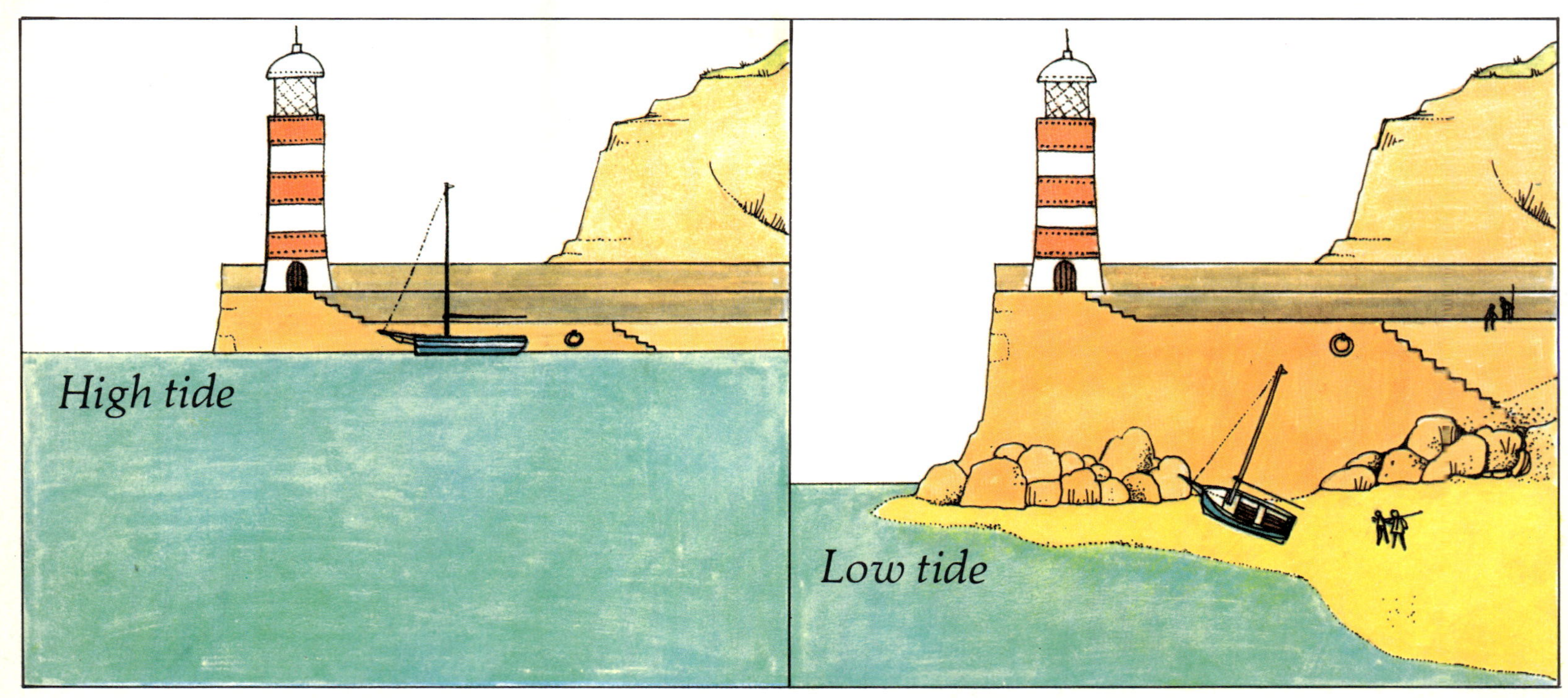

How a herring grows up

A female herring lays thousands of eggs or spawn.

The eggs hatch into larvae.

The larvae swim near the shore and turn into whitebait.

A herring is fully grown when it is 1-2 years old.

Boats and ships

These ships have engines

paddle steamer

liner

tug

motor boat

cargo ship

tanker

submarine

Making a sailing boat

Cut the hull from balsa wood.

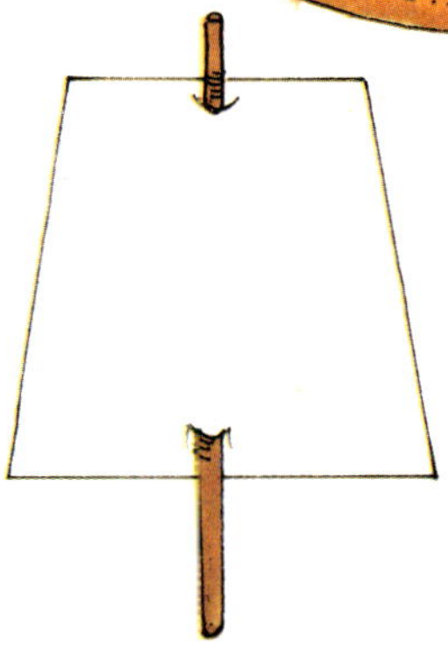

Make a paper sail on a stick.

Fix the mast to the hull.

Try different shaped sails.

Making a paddle steamer

Cut the hull from balsa wood.

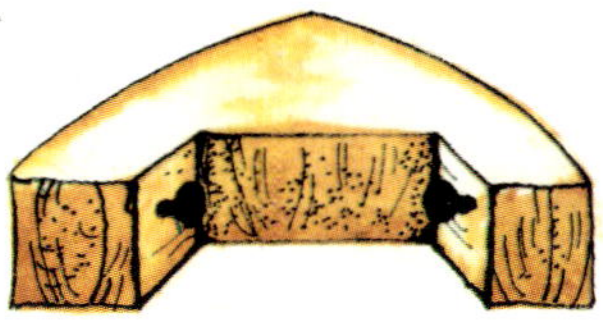

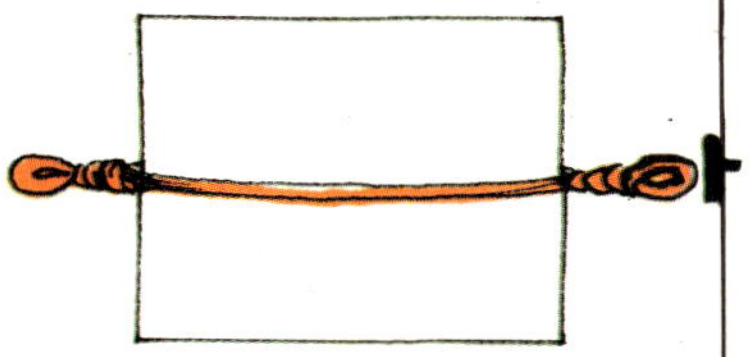

Fix a card in an elastic band to two nails.

Wind up the elastic band. As it unwinds the boat moves.

Inside a ship

A ship is a very busy place.
It has engines that move it through the water.
It carries people and cargo all over the world.

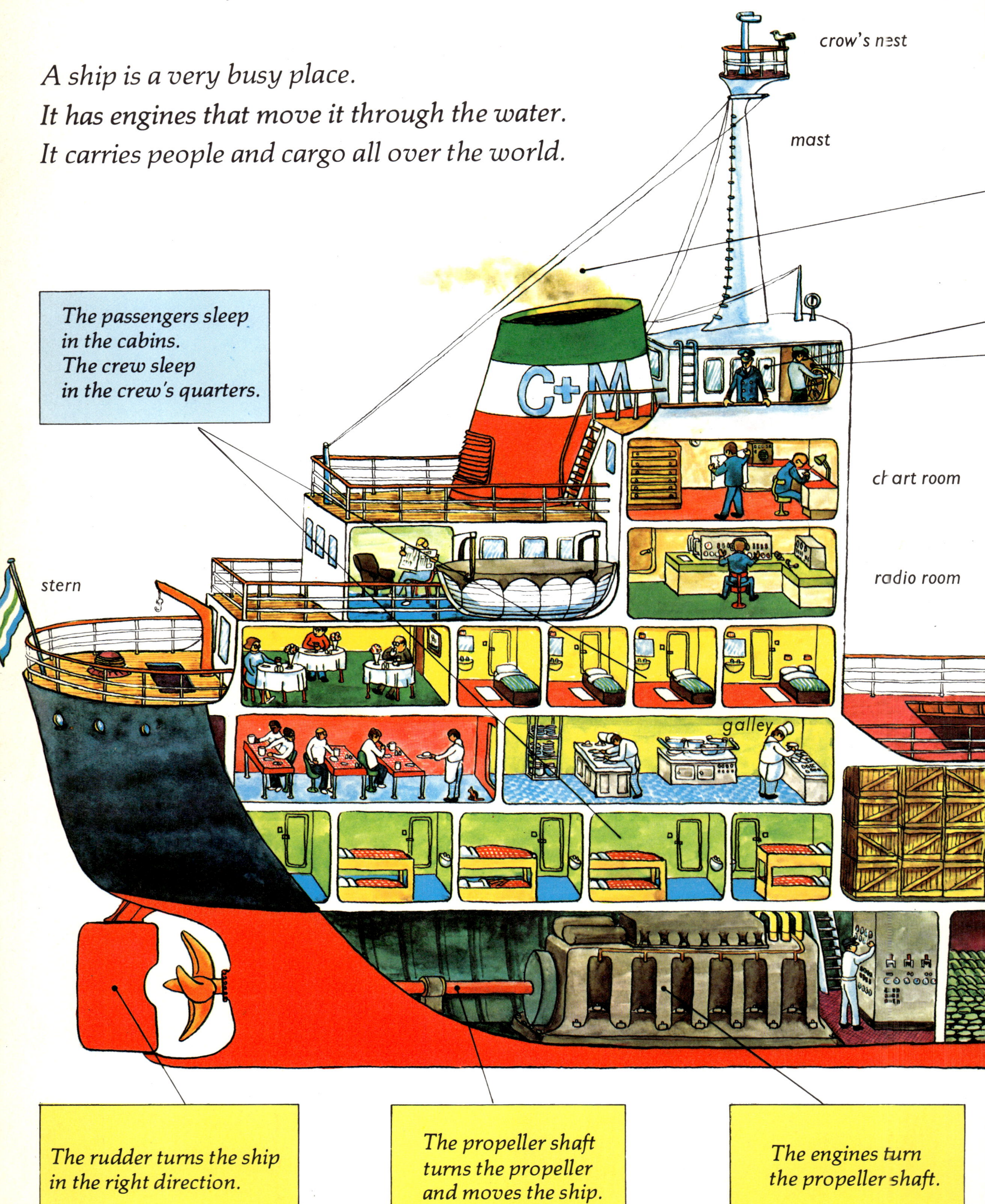

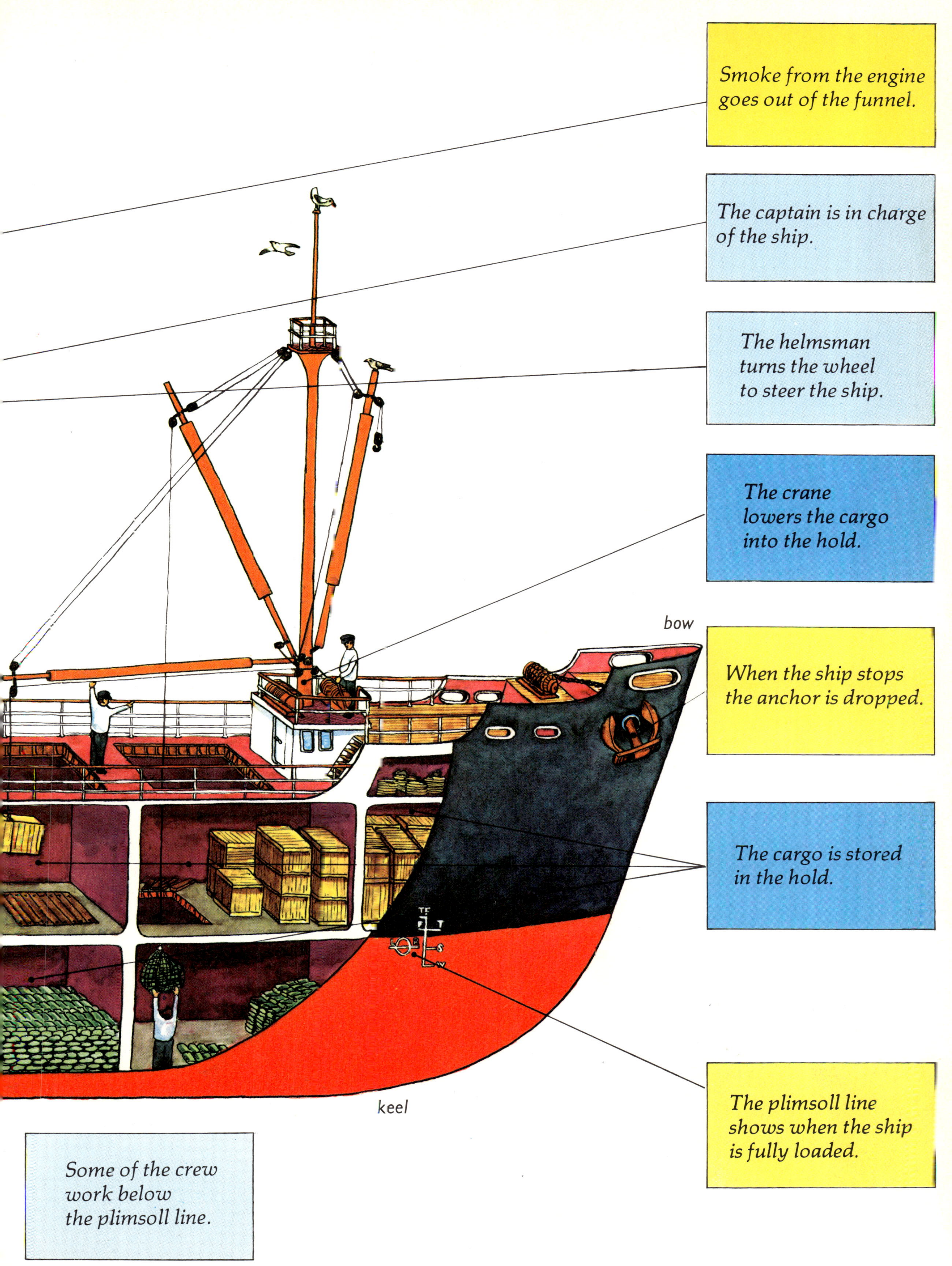
Smoke from the engine goes out of the funnel.
The captain is in charge of the ship.
The helmsman turns the wheel to steer the ship.
The crane lowers the cargo into the hold.
bow
When the ship stops the anchor is dropped.
The cargo is stored in the hold.
keel
The plimsoll line shows when the ship is fully loaded.
Some of the crew work below the plimsoll line.

Up in the air

Making a paper glider

1 Fold a piece of paper in half.

2 Fold the ends up on both sides.

3 Fold both sides up again.

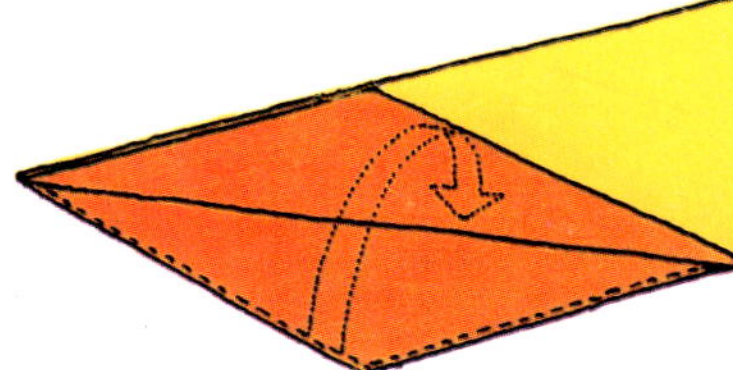

4 Fold both sides down.

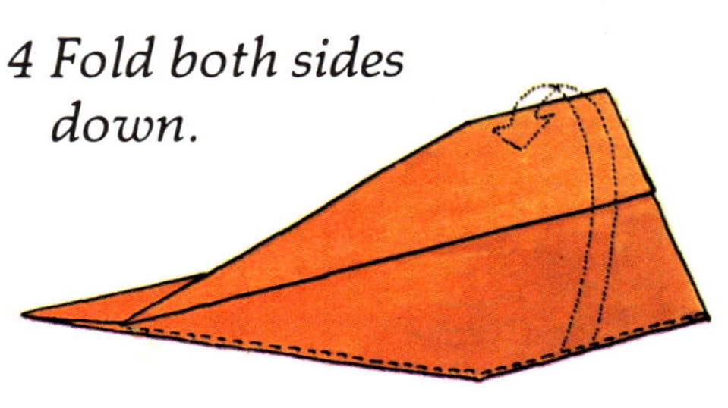

5 Fly your glider.

Making a paper propeller

On an aeroplane the propeller pushes the air back.

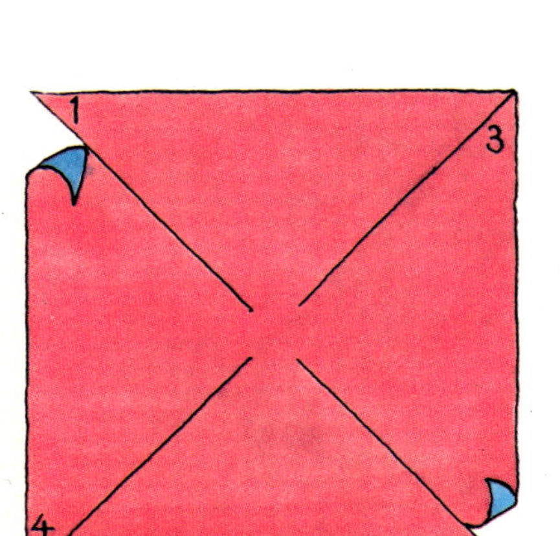

Take a square of paper.
Cut lines toward the centre.

Fold corners 1, 2, 3 and 4 to the back.

Pin the propeller onto a stick.

A jet-propelled balloon

Blow up a balloon.
Let it fly away.

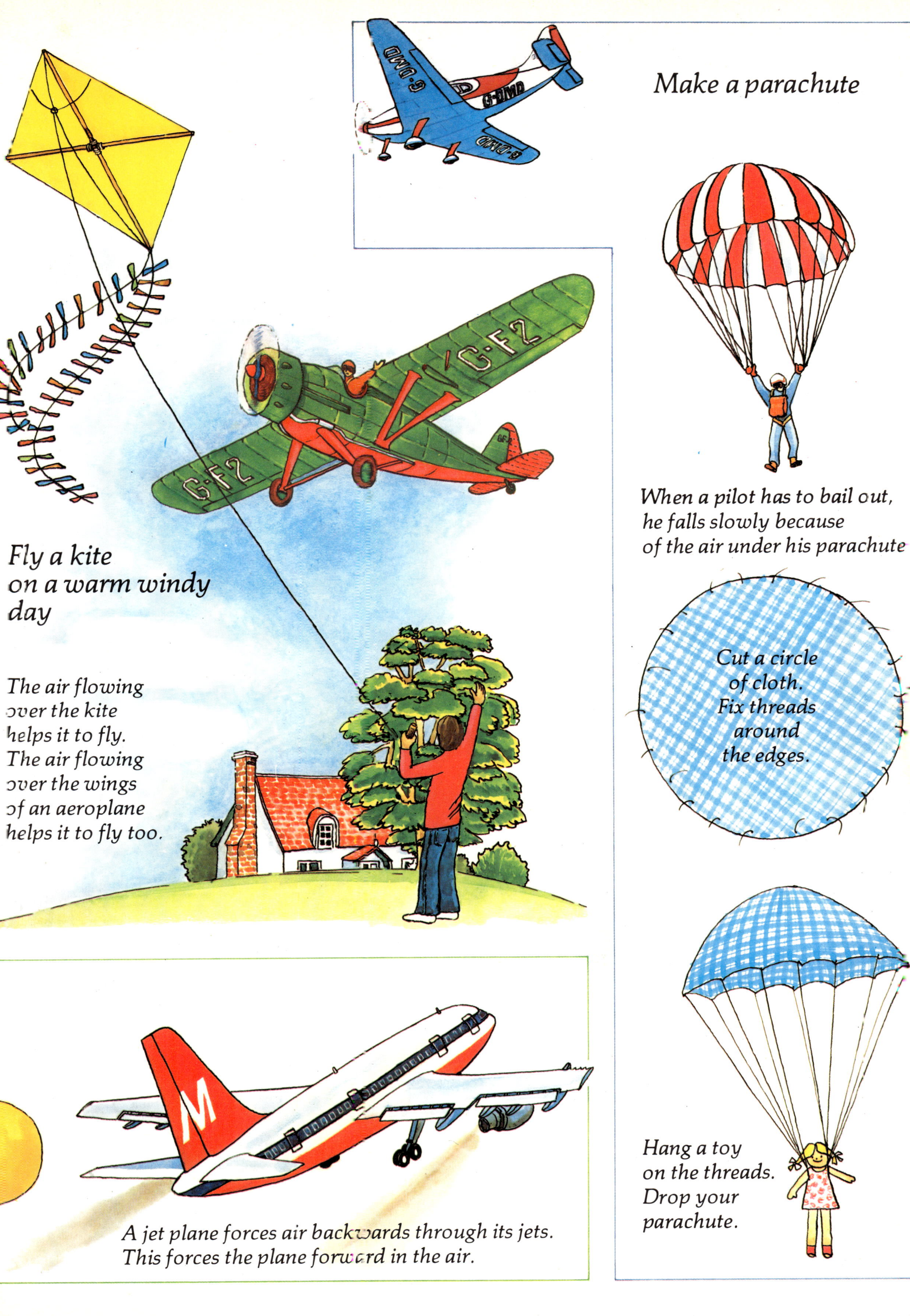

Fly a kite on a warm windy day

The air flowing over the kite helps it to fly. The air flowing over the wings of an aeroplane helps it to fly too.

A jet plane forces air backwards through its jets. This forces the plane forward in the air.

Make a parachute

When a pilot has to bail out, he falls slowly because of the air under his parachute

Cut a circle of cloth. Fix threads around the edges.

Hang a toy on the threads. Drop your parachute.

How we travel

We travel along roads

We walk slowly.

We go fast on bicycles.

We travel on water

rowing boat

yacht

We travel along tracks

Monorail trains go along overhead tracks.

Trams go along tracks

Trains go along tracks through the country.

Underground trains go on tracks through tunnels under cities.

The end of the journey

Which kind of transport ends in each place?

Airport

Bus depot

Station

Harbour

How plants grow

Parts of a plant

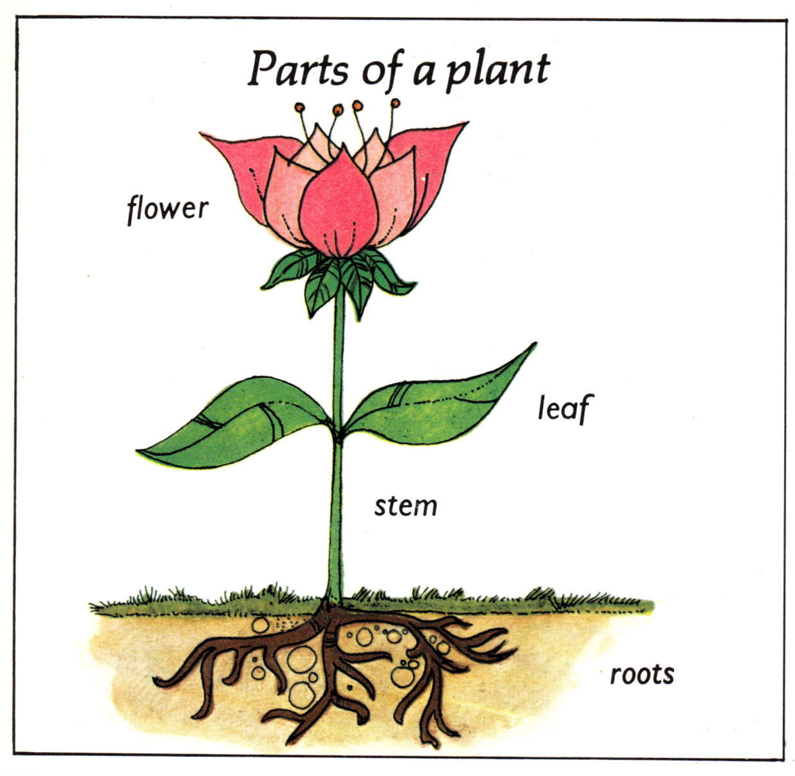

What plants need to make them grow

How seeds move around

Watching a seed grow

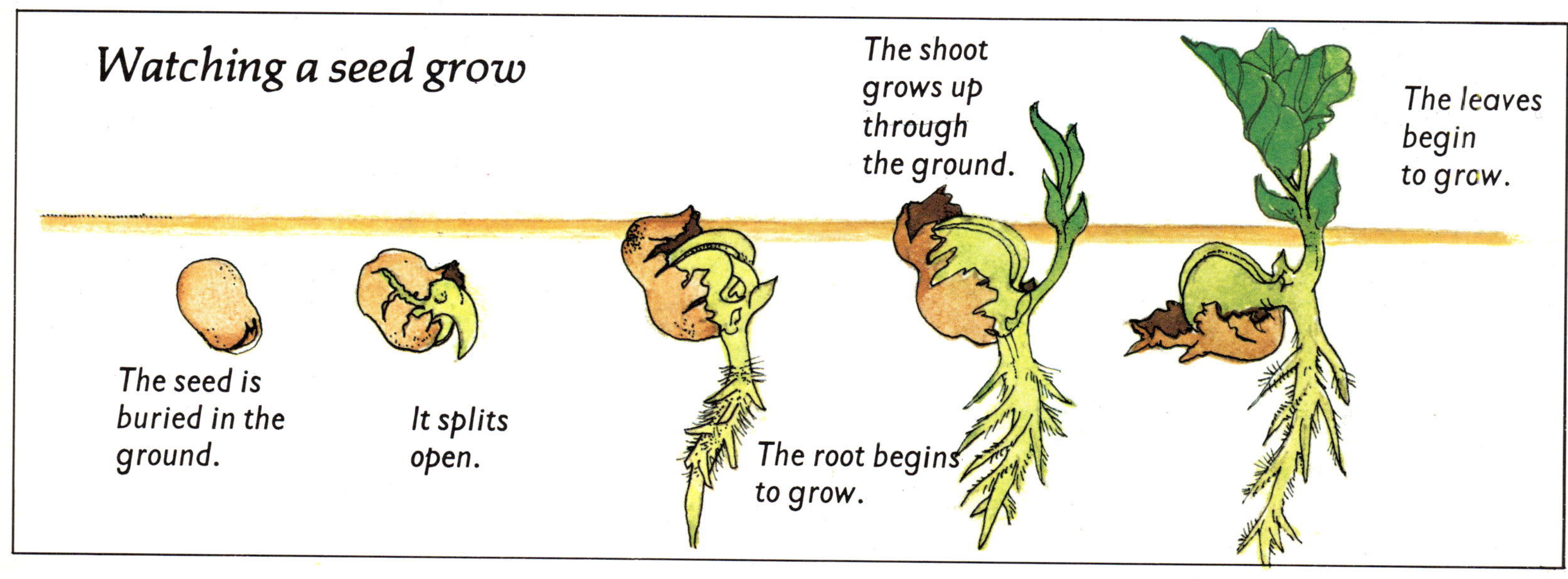

Do you know these flowers?

Trees have different leaves

A tree through the year

Growing vegetable tops

Cut the tops off root vegetables.

Stand them in a saucer of water.

Watch them sprout.

More about plants

Plants have different seeds.

Bees carry a fine dust called pollen from flower to flower. The pollen helps to make new flowers grow.

Plants have different roots.

Pick a budding twig in the spring. Put it in water and watch it grow.

Some leaves change colour in the autumn.

Evergreens are green all through the year.

Grow a plant from a bulb

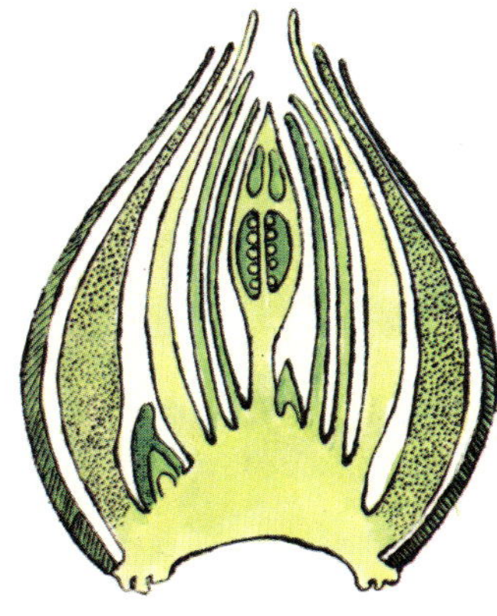

Inside this bulb the plant is ready to grow.

Put the bulb in some earth. Keep it in a dark place until the leaves begin to show.

Bring the bowl out on to a sunny windowsill. Watch your plant grow.

How we use plants

We use different parts of many plants.

Parts of a plant

We use these leaves.

We eat these roots.

We use flowers for decoration and to make scent.

We use the trunks of trees to make furniture.

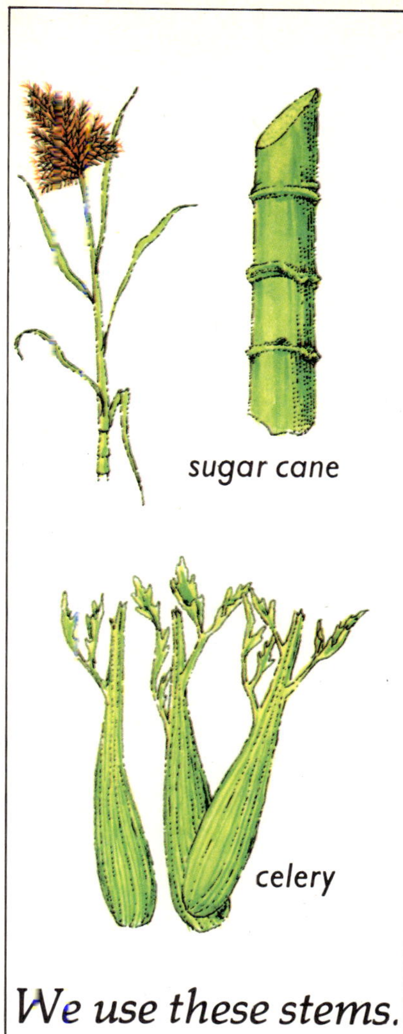

We use these stems.

We eat seeds and nuts.

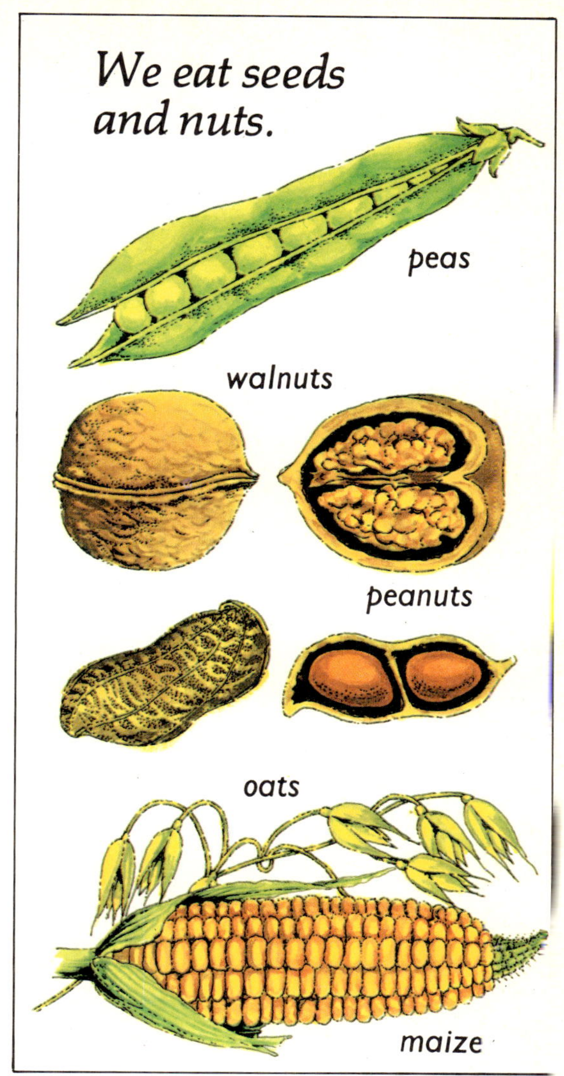

We eat these fruits.

We use these berries.

What happens on the farm

There are different kinds of farms in different parts of the world.

Growing wheat in Canada

Growing grapes in France

Growing sugar-cane in Jamaica

Sheep farming in Australia

Growing rice in China

Growing tulips in Holland

Machines used on a farm

Tractor

Milking machine

ectric shears

Combine harvester

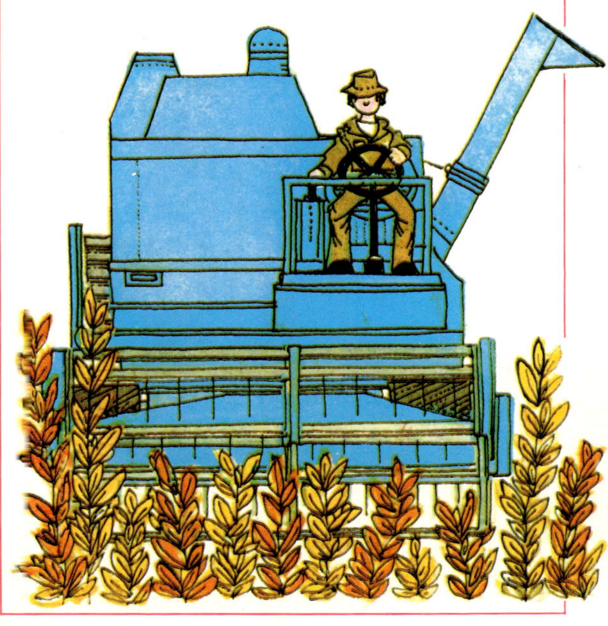

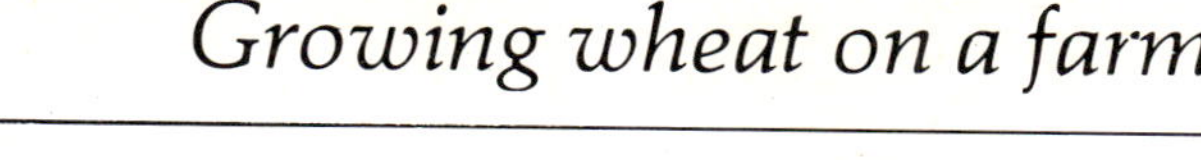

Growing wheat on a farm

The ploughed field is seeded.

The crop is sprayed to kill pests.

The wheat is harvested.

The food we eat

Who eats what?

Animals that eat meat are carnivores.

Animals that eat plants are herbivores.

What one owl catches in a year:

2000 mice

450 voles

400 birds

100 frogs

250 worms

150 snails

Make sugar mice

1. Sieve 225 grams (8 ounces) of icing sugar.
2. Mix 1 teaspoon glucose into 1 tablespoon of boiling water.
3. Mix the icing sugar slowly into the water.
4. Knead the mixture to make it smooth.
5. Shape into mice with thin string tails.

Where does your food come from?

urope
Asia
frica
Australia
apples
spices
coconuts
coffee
tea
rice
pineapples
butter
grapefruit
lemons
figs
dates
bananas
grapes
oranges
apricots
tomatoes
honey

How your body works

Parts of your body

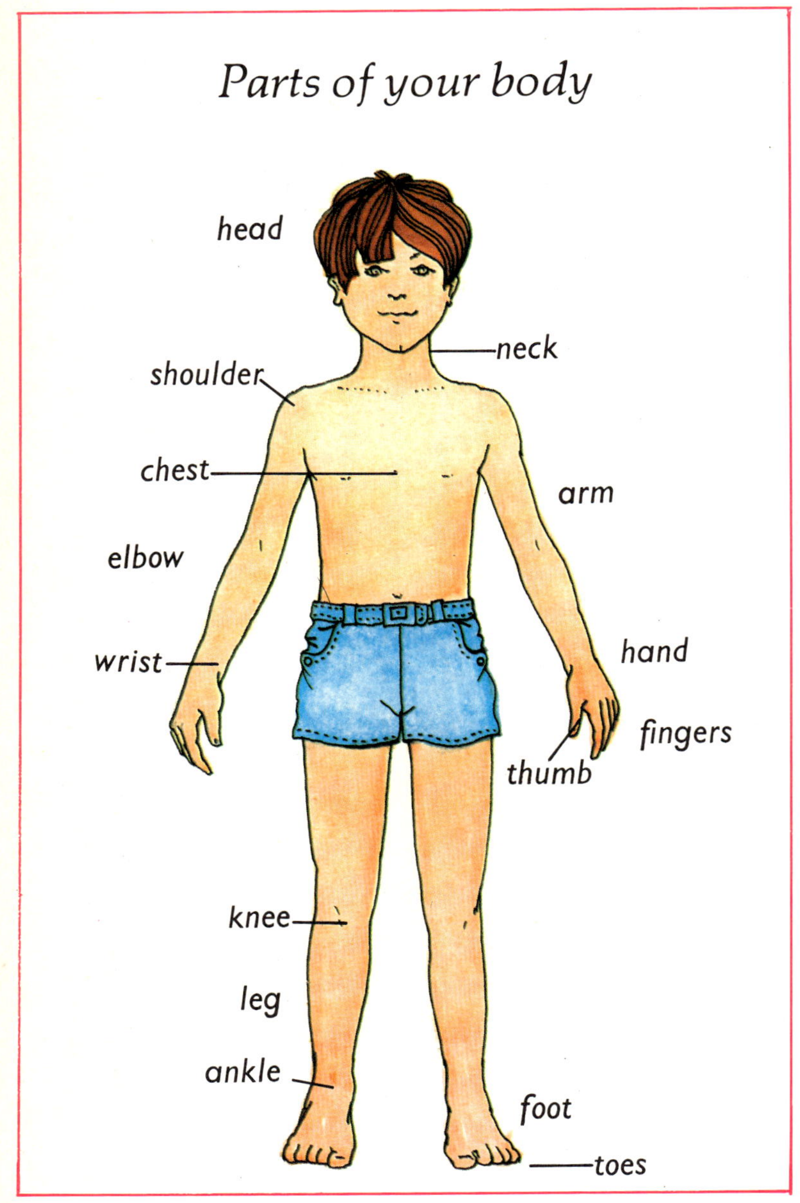

The bones of your skeleton

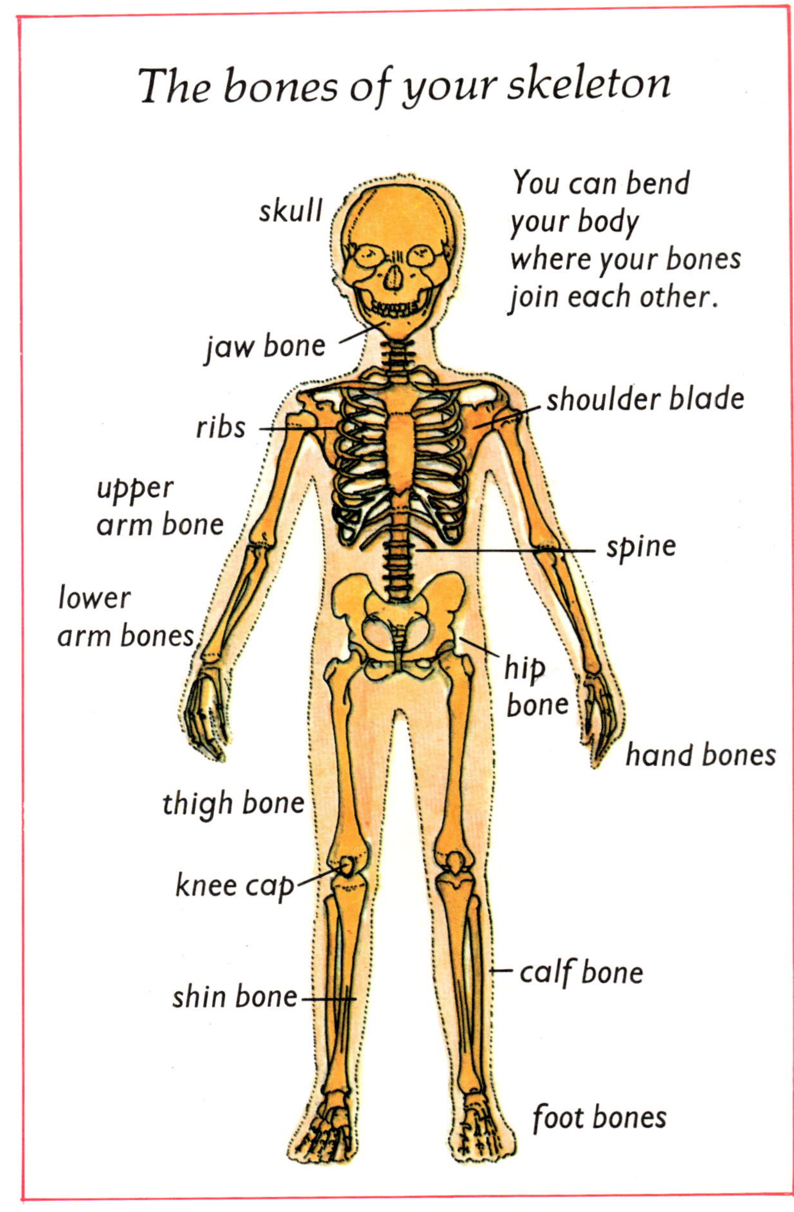

You have five senses to tell your body things.

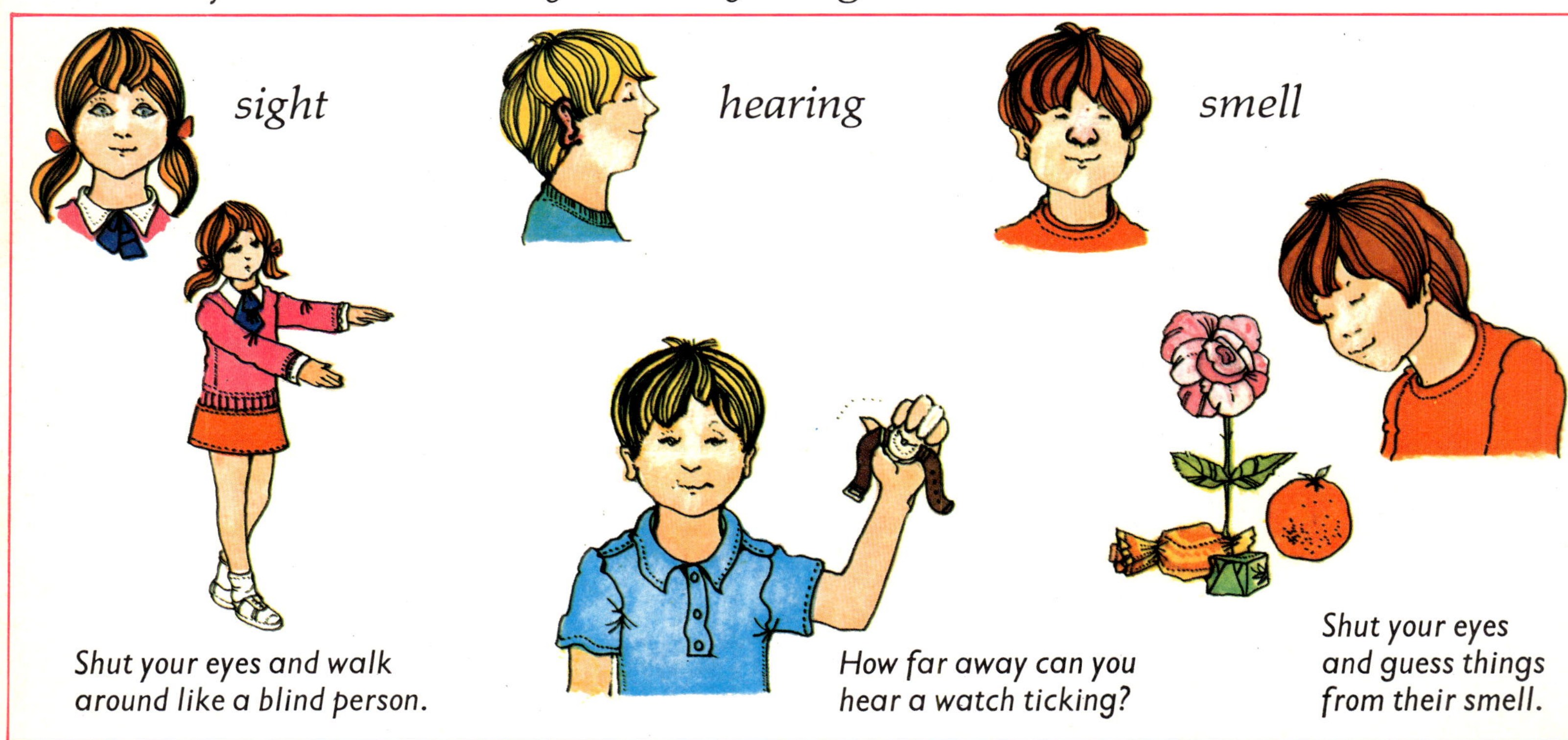

Inside your body

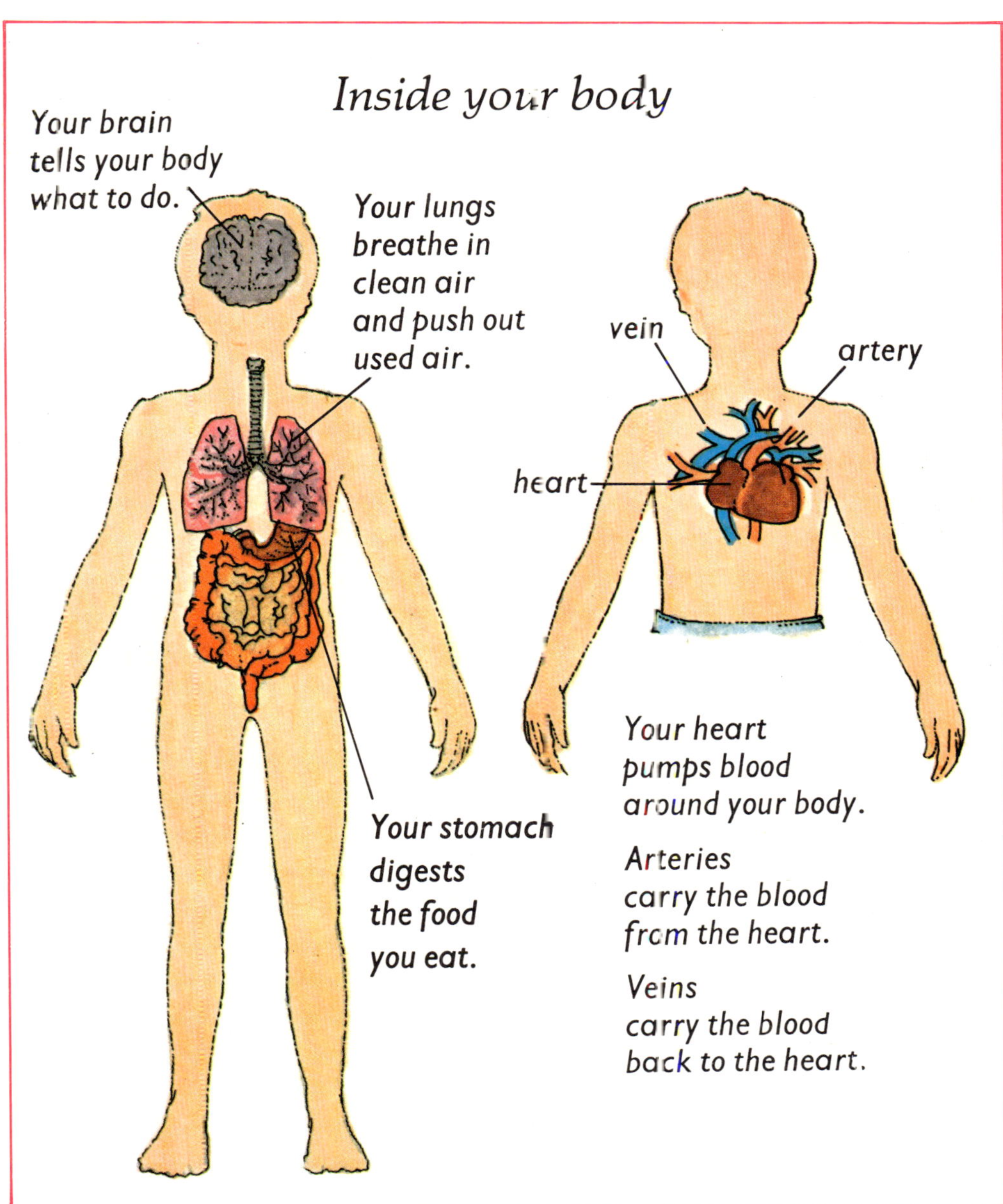

Your brain tells your body what to do.

Your lungs breathe in clean air and push out used air.

Your stomach digests the food you eat.

Your heart pumps blood around your body.

Arteries carry the blood from the heart.

Veins carry the blood back to the heart.

Put six things in a bag. Guess what they are by feeling.

Choose between salt and sugar with your eyes shut.

What you need to make you healthy

You need sleep.

You need to eat these foods.

You need exercise.

The sounds we hear

Listen to the sounds around you.
Some are loud and some are soft.

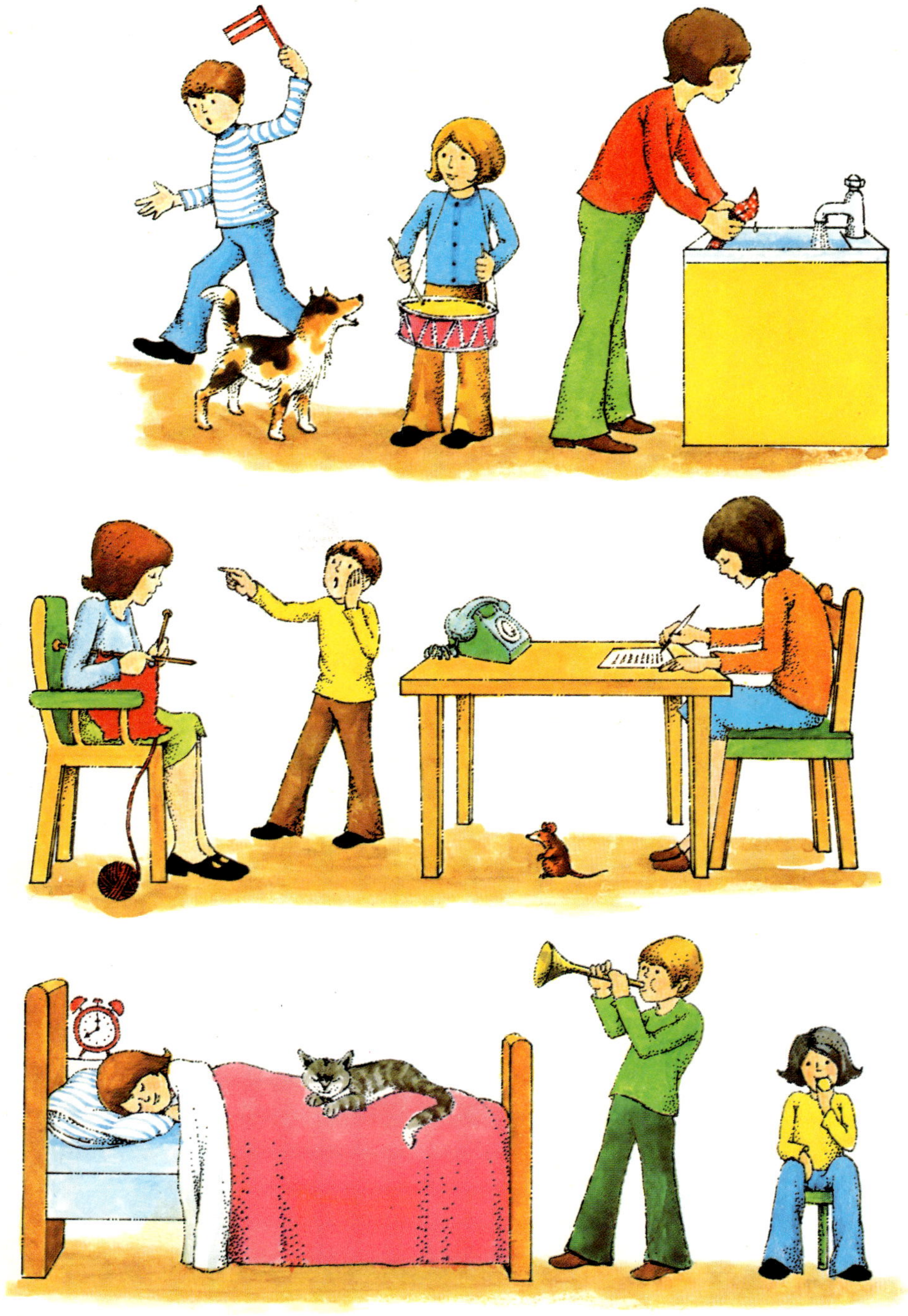

People speak many different languages.

We use sounds in many ways

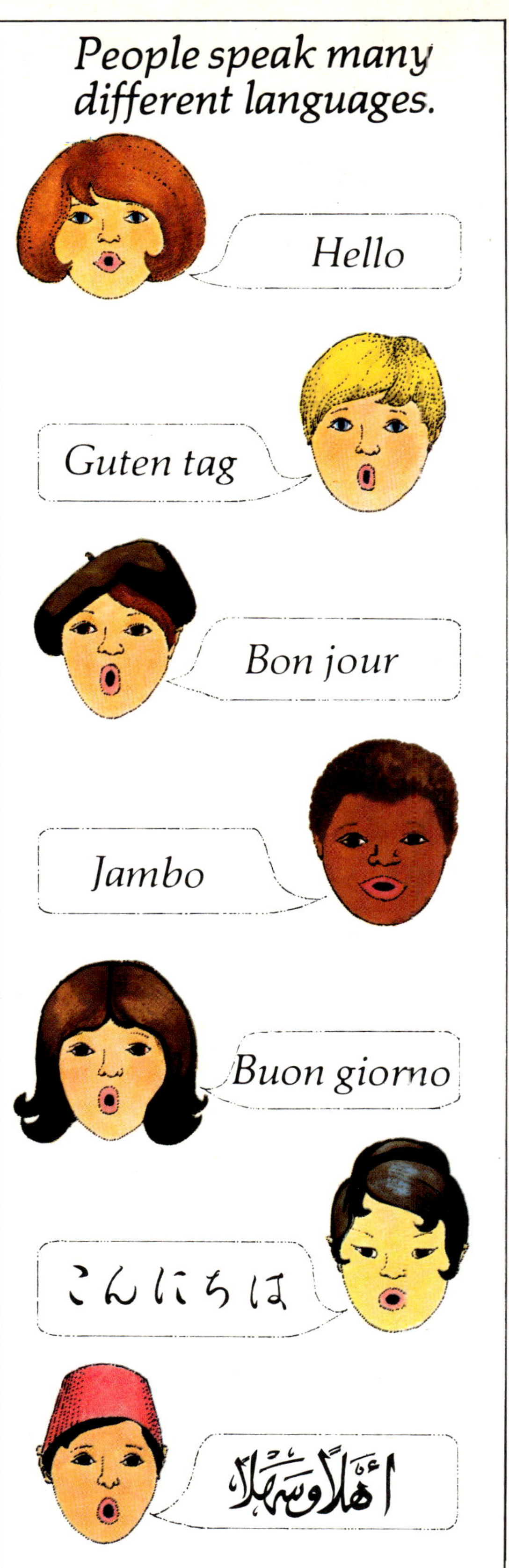

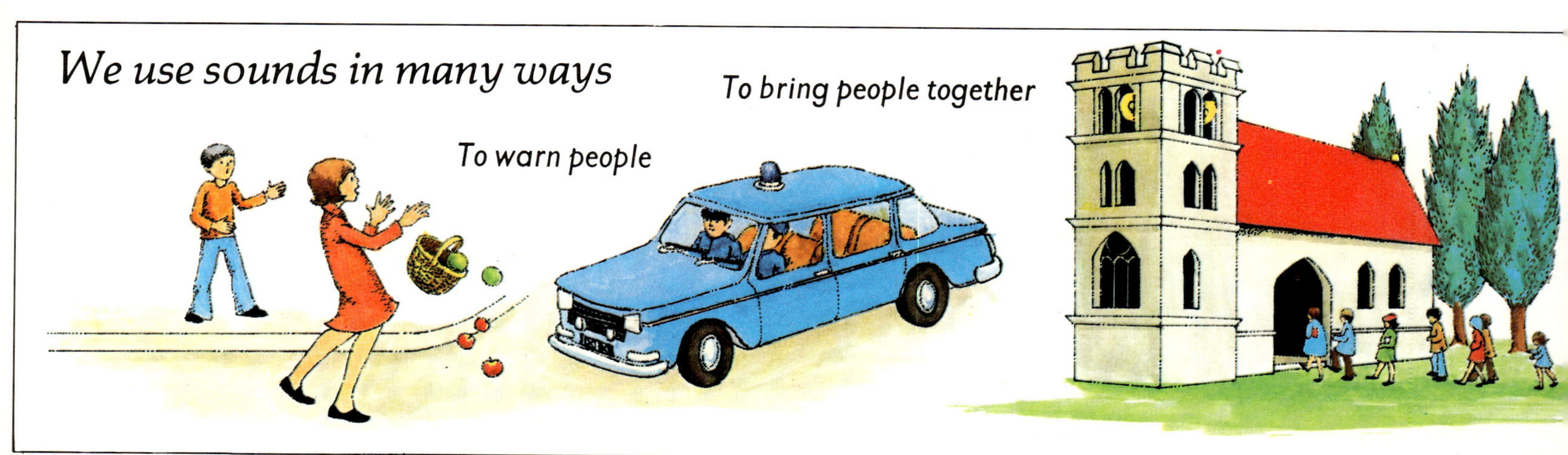

Making things to make a noise

Shaker stick

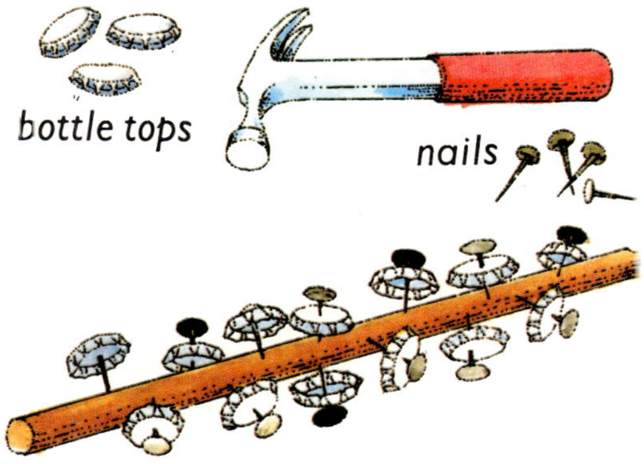
bottle tops
nails

Telephone

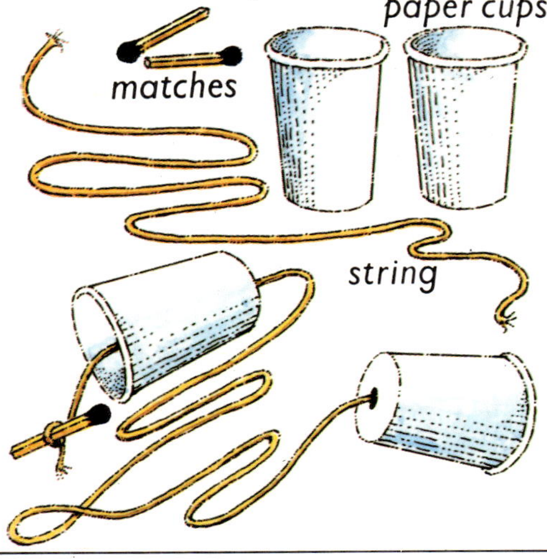
paper cups
matches
string

Bottle blower

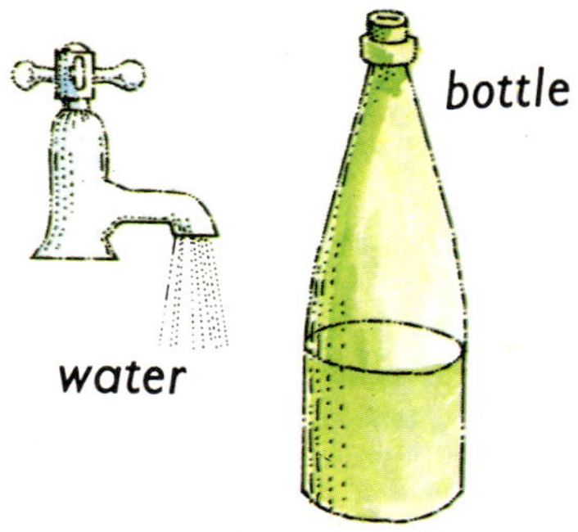
bottle
water

Spoons

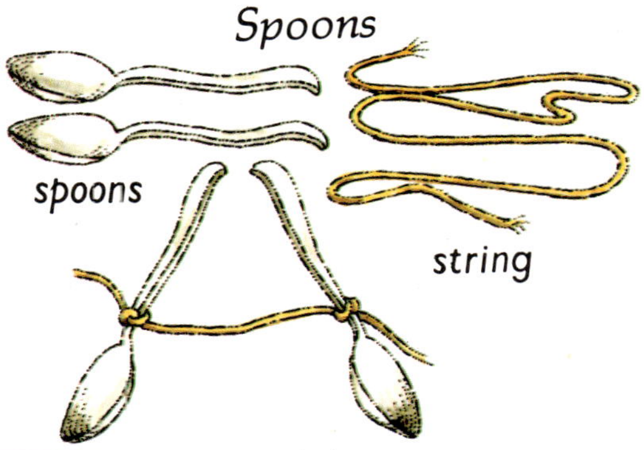
spoons
string

Bottle xylophone

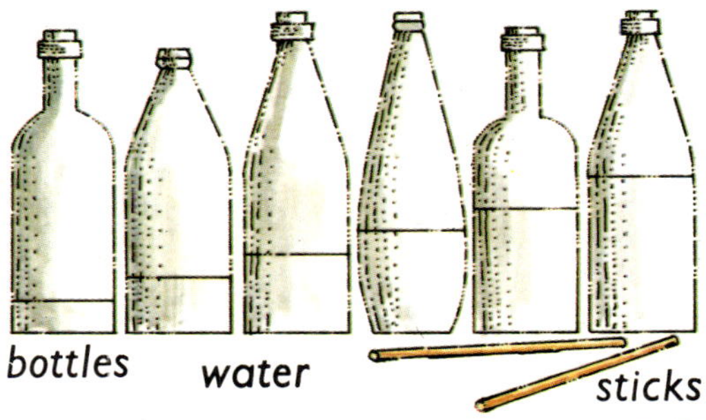
bottles
water
sticks

Box guitar

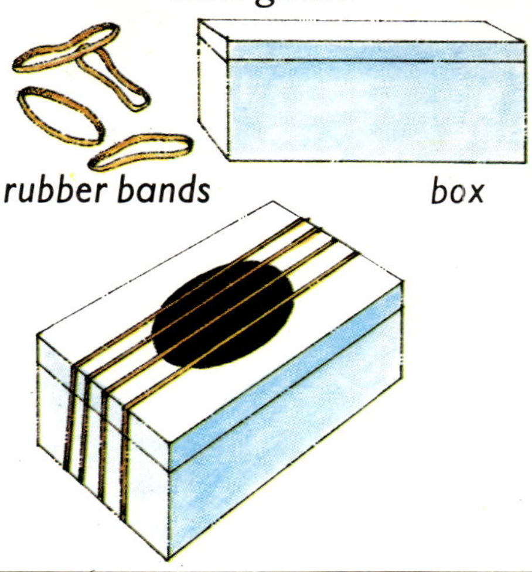
rubber bands
box

Shaker

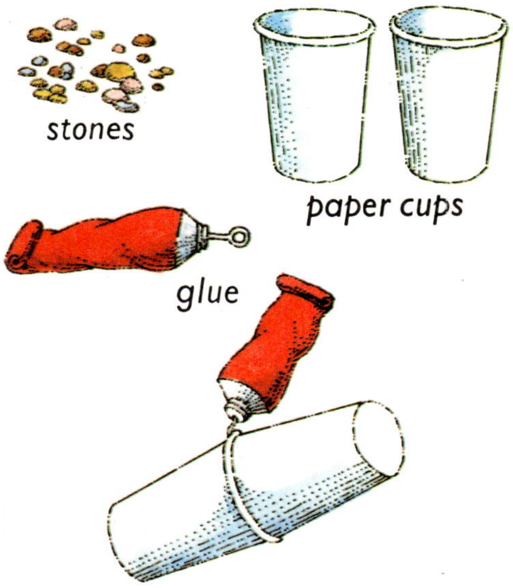
stones
paper cups
glue

To talk to each other

To make music

To call people

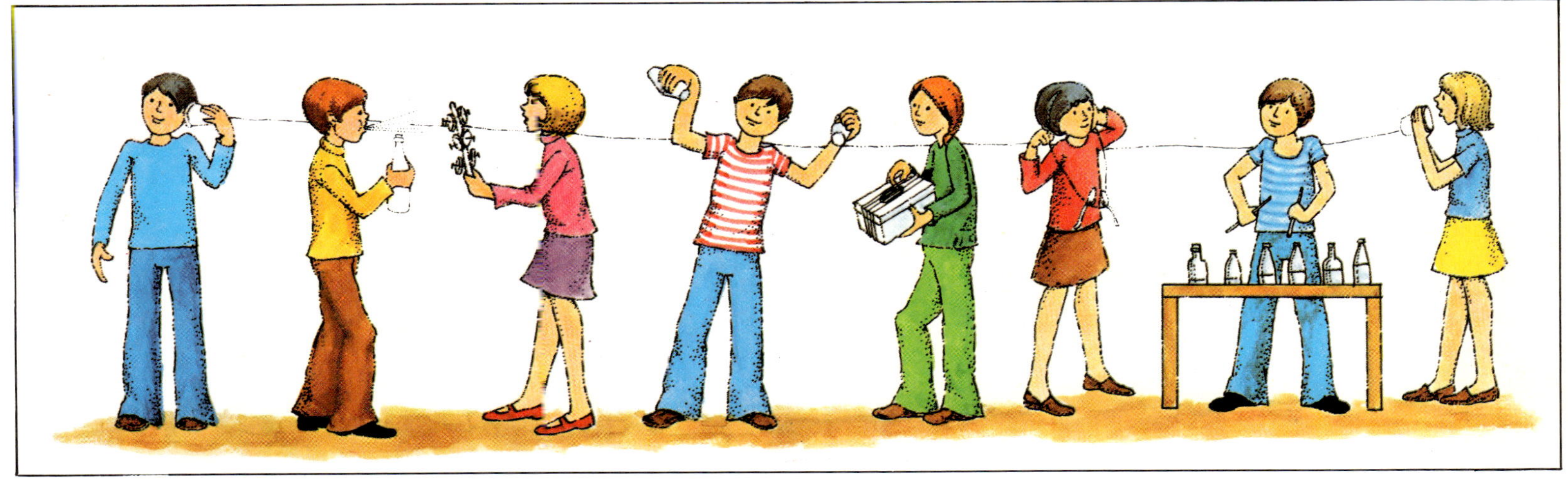

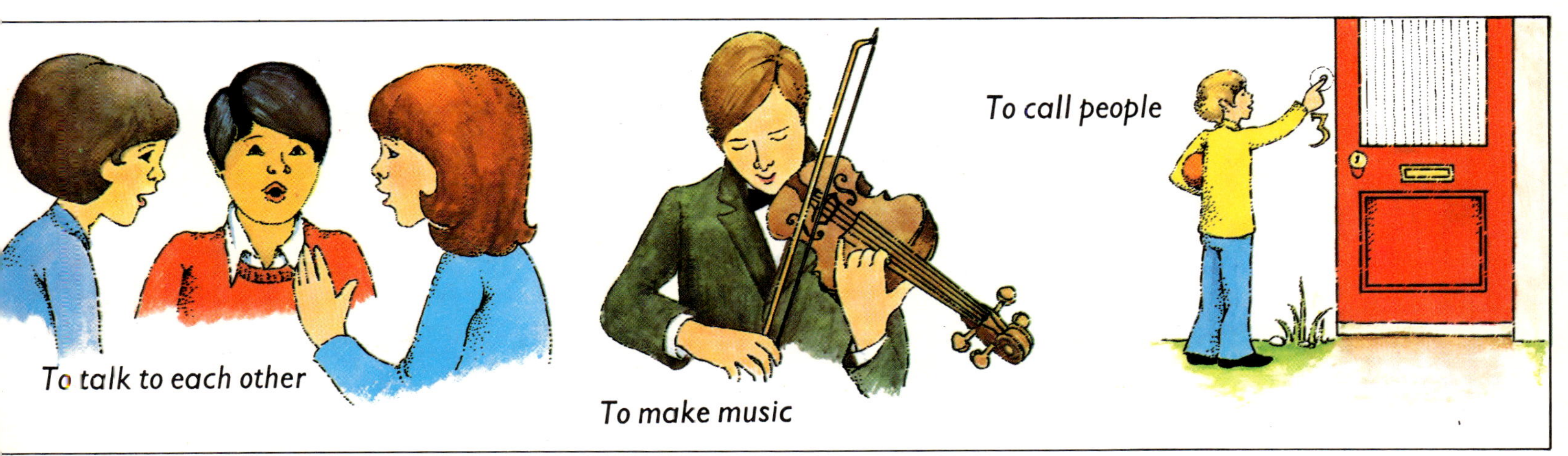

Finding is fun

What are the names of these things? If you do not know, you can look up the answers in the book. The numbers tell you which page to look at.

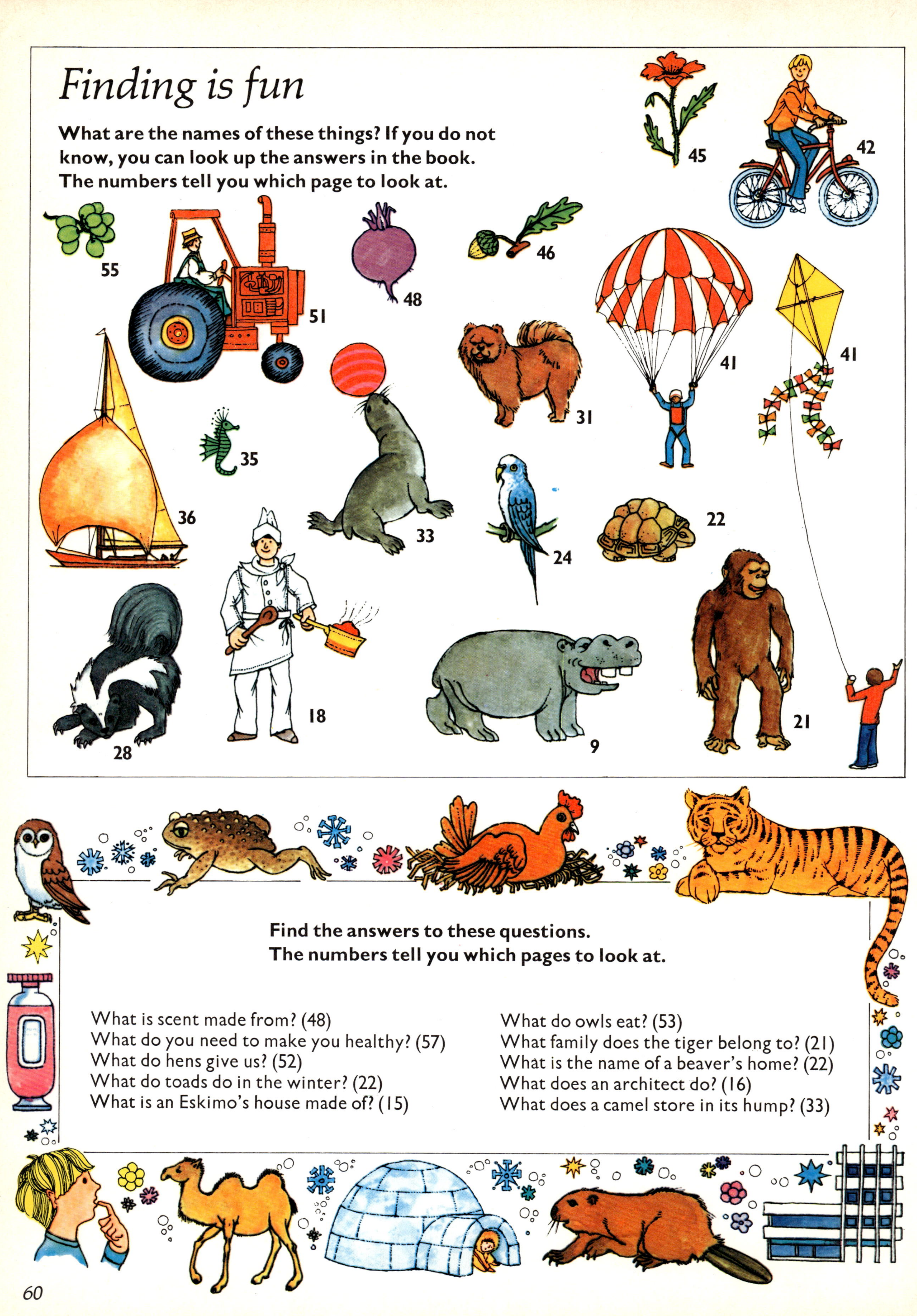

Find the answers to these questions. The numbers tell you which pages to look at.

What is scent made from? (48)
What do you need to make you healthy? (57)
What do hens give us? (52)
What do toads do in the winter? (22)
What is an Eskimo's house made of? (15)

What do owls eat? (53)
What family does the tiger belong to? (21)
What is the name of a beaver's home? (22)
What does an architect do? (16)
What does a camel store in its hump? (33)

Find the odd one out

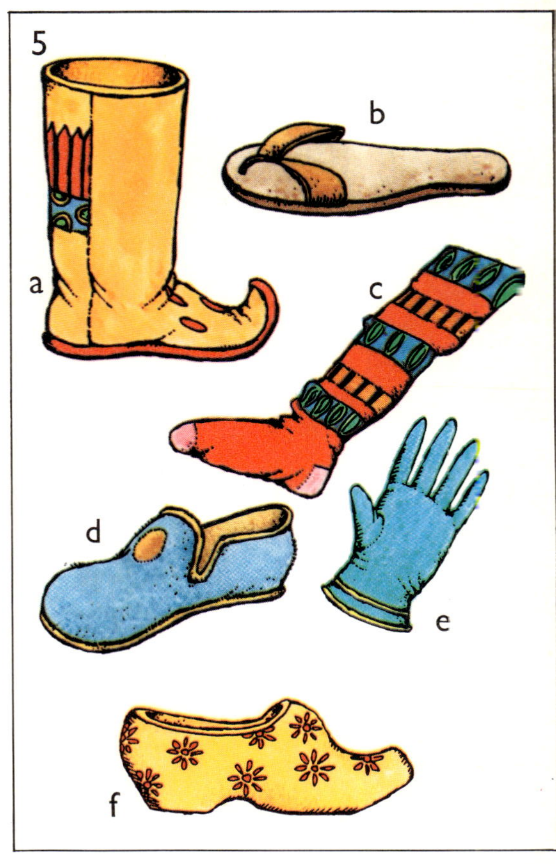

The odd ones are:

1 c The poppy is a flower, not a vegetable.

2 e The hedgehog lives on land, not in the sea.

3 c The submarine travels under water, not on the surface.

4 b The butterfly is an insect, not a bird.

5 e The glove is worn on your hand, not on your foot.

6 c The dog does not belong to the cat family.

These are the pairs:

camel and desert
fishing boat and fisherman
igloo and Eskimo
gypsy and caravan
butterfly and caterpillar
tepee and American Indian